AMERICA THROUGH FOREIGN EYES

1827–1842

AMERICA
THROUGH FOREIGN EYES
1827-1842

SELECTED SOURCE MATERIALS
FOR FRESHMAN RESEARCH PAPERS

Edited by
ROLAND BARTEL *and* EDWIN R. BINGHAM
UNIVERSITY OF OREGON

D. C. HEATH AND COMPANY *Boston*

PRINTED IN THE UNITED STATES OF AMERICA (5 K 5)

TABLE OF CONTENTS

INTRODUCTION

The Research Paper

One of the most useful skills you can acquire in college is that of organizing your ideas on a given topic and developing them into a finished paper. Whether you are preparing a written assignment, answering examination questions, writing a report in your business or profession, or simply trying to think in an orderly manner, you will find this skill invaluable.

Learning to write a research paper will help you develop this ability to organize and present an assortment of ideas effectively because a research paper requires you to collect and evaluate the information for your subject from a variety of sources. Instead of relying on your own supply of experiences and opinions, as you do in most weekly themes, you consult other authorities, bring together the facts and opinions you consider most valuable, and present them in the way that seems most meaningful to you. Thus the research paper gives you an opportunity to impose your own pattern upon the unsystematized materials which your investigation has produced.

It is well to distinguish at once between two types of material that are used in most research papers, namely, primary and secondary. Primary materials are the first hand observations and reflections that are not based on other written works. They are still in their original form, not having been organized or interpreted by someone else. Diaries, letters, reports, and similar documents are the best examples of primary materials, but in a broader sense, any material that gives the researcher the facts for his paper without helping him solve his problems of organization and interpretation may be considered primary in nature. Secondary materials are those innumerable books and articles which discuss the written works of others. They are called secondary because they stand between you and the original sources and often give you the interpretations that you are trying to make for yourself. Lincoln's letters would be primary materials. An article on Lincoln's sense of humor as revealed in his letters would be secondary material.

The ideal way to begin your training in research is to base your first papers on primary materials. This will enable you to plan and write your own paper without being distracted by someone else's discussion of your topic. You will learn to use your own judgment as you evaluate your sources, collect your notes, draw up your own outline, form your own conclusions, and write your own original report. You will develop the quality of self-reliance which will prepare you to use both primary and secondary sources properly in your future papers.

This book provides you the primary materials for a variety of research papers. It contains first hand accounts of foreign travelers in the United States between the years 1827 and 1842. The "Age of Jackson," as one historian has named the period, seems to have presented to the Old World traveler sometimes admirable, sometimes disgusting, but nearly always vital and varied scenes upon which to comment. Americans in the 1830's were a restless, optimistic, self-assertive people well on the way to achieving a cultural independence to match the political independence that the War of 1812 had reinforced. They were busy moving west, making money, building roads, getting elected, and expending their energies prodigiously, propelled and encouraged all the while by a widespread conviction of their social and political equality. The common man had never felt so important or been so powerful; nor, in the opinion of certain observers, had he ever been so common.

The observations of American life recorded by travelers from abroad have been reprinted in this book as they were written in the nineteenth century, except that the use of italics and quotation marks has been standardized. Spelling and punctuation have been left unchanged. The page numbers of the original books have been inserted in the margins so that you can refer to them in your footnotes. The omission of parts of the material has been indicated by spaced periods.

In writing research papers from this book you will follow essentially the same procedure as you will in future papers based on other sources. You will survey the available material, choose a topic, make a tentative outline, collect your notes, revise your outline, and write and rewrite your paper. You will have the advantage of being able to concentrate on these basic problems of research writing before you take on the additional task of learning to use the facilities of the library, the subject of the last section of this book. By mastering the principles of research writing and the use of the library in two separate steps, you should be able to do a better job of both.

The Topic

In order to choose a topic as intelligently as possible, you should do some exploratory reading in all parts of this collection. This will give you a general familiarity with the background and open up many subjects for research. It will give you the "feel" of Jacksonian America and make you aware that you are behind the scenes in an interesting period in history. You will discover that you are dealing with the raw materials from which real history is written, and that your research will add to your understanding both of history and of literature. In your future library papers this first step will include making a tentative bibliography as described in the final section of this book.

After you have completed your preliminary reading, you should choose a topic and phrase it carefully to indicate precisely what you intend to cover. Learning to adjust the topic to the specified length of the paper and to the available resources is so important that you should get all the help you can from your rhetoric book and from your instructor.

The Outline

After you have surveyed your material and chosen your topic, you should make a trial outline. You should always remember that your first outline is a tentative one. Many students ruin their papers by clinging stubbornly to their original outlines. The final outline must be made inductively; that is, it must reflect what you discover to be important rather than what you considered to be important at the start. You should think about the organization of your paper in all stages of your reading, but you should not make the final outline until you have collected all your material and evaluated it carefully. Follow the outlining techniques recommended by your instructor.

Note Cards

It would be possible to write short papers based on this book without the use of note cards. But to write the longer papers, and even some of the shorter ones, you will find it advantageous to make note cards. You will save time in this way because all the material on your particular subject, which is scattered throughout the book (or throughout the library in your future papers) will then lie before you in small units. You can bring together the cards on different parts of your subject and fit the material logically into your outline or rearrange it to conform to last minute changes. You will do a better job on your paper because making note cards gives you a better opportunity to analyze your material carefully.

Every note card should be limited to a single topic. This is basic because one purpose of these notes is to enable you to study your material in several different arrangements. In addition, every card should contain three parts: a subject heading, composed by you, placed in the upper left-hand corner; the source, including the page number, in the upper right-hand corner or at the bottom; and the body of the note itself. Placing both the subject heading and the source at the top leaves the bottom of the card open for your own comments which you may wish to add.

The subject heading should be a catch word or phrase which identifies the contents of the card accurately. Such general headings as "Jackson admired" or "Jackson criticized" would be less useful than more specific ones, such as "Jackson's manner admired" or "Jackson critical of France." You will often have several cards with identical subject headings, but this should occur only when the contents of the cards are on the same specific point.

The source can be identified by abbreviating the author and title if all your sources are before you in one book as they are in this instance or if you have complete bibliography cards for each source you propose to use. The page number (and volume number in multi-volume works) must always be included.

The body of the note may take one of two basic forms: it may be written in your own words or it may be quoted directly from the source. It is highly desirable that most of your note cards for your first few research papers be written in your own words to give you more practice in composition and to avoid the kind of paper that merely strings together quotations. If you take pains to write the notes well, you will have a much easier time writing the first draft of your paper.

The length of your note cards will vary according to the length and importance of the material you are recording. Most frequently you will find it desirable to summarize or condense the source, but occasionally you may find a passage that is so vital to your paper that you cannot condense it. Then you will want to paraphrase it, that is, rewrite it in your own words without shortening it very much. When writing your own note cards, either in the form of summaries or paraphrases, you must be careful to develop your own style and to avoid plagiarism or near plagiarism. It is inevitable that you will repeat some of the words found in the source, but you should develop your own phrasing and sentence structure. If you were writing a paper on the condition of the Negro slave in the South, you would record on one card (see next page) Charles Augustus Murray's observations on the plight of the farm-laboring Negro in Virginia (p. 96).

Although you should use direct quotations sparingly in your first paper, you should learn to use them correctly. When you quote directly you must be scrupulously accurate. There is no such thing as a near quotation; you must either quote

Condition of farm-laboring slave — Murray, I, 167-168

Murray points out that the farm-laboring slave is in a particularly unenviable position because of several related reasons: he has little contact with the master of the plantation; he is one of a gang from which a specific quota of work is demanded; he is subject to the authority of an overseer, generally, Murray feels, a man of harsh and callous character, whose prime concern is to get the work out; and he has no effective recourse to the master since Negro testimony is largely ignored

Note to yourself → Remember to contrast the plight of the farm-laboring slave with the easier circumstances of the domestic slave as described elsewhere in Murray's account.

exactly or not at all. You should observe the following rules rigidly, both in your note cards and in your paper:

1. The source must be reproduced exactly, including punctuation marks and misspellings.
2. The quoted part must be enclosed in quotation marks if it does not exceed four lines; if it is longer, it should be indented without the use of quotation marks.
3. Ellipses marks must be used to indicate omissions within a quotation, three spaced periods for part of a sentence and four for more than a sentence.
4. Any material inserted by you must be enclosed in square brackets. It may be necessary to supply the antecedent of a pronoun: "He [the overseer] owned he was extremely sorry that the race existed in Virginia, . . ." When the quoted part contains an error the student may insert the correction immediately following it or he may insert the word *sic* (Latin for "thus") to show that he is transcribing it accurately: "Jackson arrived in Washingtin [sic] on Friday." Archaic and foreign spellings need not be pointed out.

Direct quotations should be limited to passages of unusual effectiveness and to controversial material. In a paper on the condition of the Negro slave in the South you should include a direct quotation or two reflecting Southern attitudes toward the Negro that would help you reach conclusions as to the life of the southern Negro (see sample note card on opposite page and source on page 78).

Writing the Paper

After you have completed all your note cards, you should study them carefully and make your final outline. You should not expect every card to fall neatly into place. Most cards will fit into a logical place in the outline, but a few stubborn ones will resist classification. You must be extremely cautious in dealing with these misfits. They may reveal a weakness in your organization or conclusion.

Southern white racial theory — Martineau, I, 235

While Mrs. Martineau was witnessing the sale of Negroes in a Charleston slave market a lady turned to her and said with cheerful complacency: "You know my theory, that one race must be subservient to the other. I do not care which; and if the blacks should ever have the upper hand, I should not mind standing on that table, and being sold with two of my children."

They may point to a contradiction which needs to be explained. Under no circumstances should you discard information to avoid dealing with a conflict. You may never have a better opportunity to increase your knowledge than when you wrestle with the problem of organizing facts which seem contradictory. If you cannot account for an exception to your interpretation of the facts, you should say so and let the exception stand. Throw out only those cards which are clearly irrelevant or repetitious.

After you have organized your material you should review your notes and outline until you feel confident that you can discuss your subject with authority and zest. You must never forget that the research paper is an original, creative piece of writing. It is true that you obtained your facts from your reading, but the interpretation and the presentation are original with you.

You should write the first draft with as few interruptions as possible. Do not bother about footnotes and similar details until later. This procedure is recommended as an antidote to the dull, wooden style that results from merely filling in an outline. After you have completed the first draft you should check it with the outline for digressions and omissions. You should then make corrections, add the footnotes, and rewrite as often as necessary.

The footnotes, which usually appear at the bottom of the page or at the end of the paper, are indispensable in a research paper because you must tell the reader where you got the information that is not original with you. They must be included, not only because the elementary principle of honesty requires you to acknowledge your sources, but also because you must make it possible for your reader to follow up or verify any facts in which he becomes interested.

No matter which system of documentation you use, you should see to it that all your footnotes are clear, accurate, consistent, and brief. The system standardized by the Style Sheet of the Modern Language Association has been adopted by more than seventy journals and is finding favor in many English departments. The Style Sheet can be obtained for a slight charge from the Treasurer of the MLA, 100 Washington Square, New York 3, N.Y.

The first footnote in a paper written from this book may take one of two forms. If you use the pagination of the original books, you should follow this example:

Charles Augustus Murray, *Travels in North America* (2 vols., London, 1839), I, 62.

If you use the pagination of this collection, your first footnote should follow another standard form:

Charles Augustus Murray, "Travels in North America," (London, 1839), in *America Through Foreign Eyes, 1827–1842,* eds. Roland Bartel and E.R. Bingham (Boston: Heath, 1956), p. 92.

In its final form your paper should include a title page, a copy of the outline or table of contents, a brief preface in which you explain the purpose and scope of your paper, the text of the paper including the footnotes, and a bibliography. The bibliography of a research paper is an alphabetical list of the sources used in its development. In library papers the bibliography is indispensable, but in a paper based on this book it could be omitted because it would consist of only a single entry. It would, however, be preferable to form the habit now of including a separate bibliography in all your research papers. For instructions on the correct arrangement of individual entries, see the first part of the supplement in the latter section of this book on the use of the library.

AMERICA THROUGH FOREIGN EYES
1827–1842

Frances Trollope

From *Domestic Manners of the Americans* by Mrs. Frances Trollope. Two volumes. London (Whittaker, Treacher & Co.), 1832.

Mrs. Trollope, mother of the novelist Anthony Trollope, is famous, or perhaps infamous in this country, for her caustic characterization of Jacksonian society in her *Domestic Manners of the Americans* (1832). The book was written largely to compensate for losses sustained when an attempt to establish a bazaar in Cincinnati for the sale of fancy goods failed miserably. Publication brought immediate profit and notoriety to Mrs. Trollope. As a matter of fact, in the United States the book was a best seller, suggesting that Americans in Jackson's day took pleasure in being noticed no matter how unfavorably. So well known did the book become that boorish behavior in public places might be arrested by the cry of "A Trollope! A Trollope!" Although many of Mrs. Trollope's generalizations are too sweeping and too bitter to be entirely true, there was much in American society to deserve her strictures. After writing up accounts of subsequent travels on the continent she turned to fiction. Her best known novels are *The Vicar of Wrexhill* (1837) and *Widow Barnaby* (1838). She died in Florence, Italy, in 1863.

Cincinnati — Forest Farm

I, 60 THOUGH I do not quite sympathise with those who consider Cincinnati as one of the wonders of the earth, I certainly think it a city of extraordinary size and importance, when it is remembered that thirty years ago the aboriginal forest occupied the ground where it stands; and every month appears to extend its limits and its wealth.

Some of the native political economists assert that this rapid conversion of a bear-brake into a prosperous city, is the result of free political institutions; not being very deep in such matters, a more obvious cause suggested itself to me, in the unceasing goad which necessity applies to industry in this country, and in the absence of all resource for the idle. During nearly two years that I resided in Cincinnati, or its neighbourhood, I neither saw a beggar, nor I, 61 a man of sufficient / fortune to permit his ceasing his efforts to increase it; thus every bee in the hive is actively employed in search of that honey of Hybla, vulgarly called money; neither art, science, learning, nor pleasure can seduce them from its pursuit. This unity of purpose, backed by the spirit of enterprise, and joined with an acuteness and absence of probity, where interest is concerned, which might set canny Yorkshire at defiance, may well go far towards obtaining its purpose.

The low rate of taxation, too, unquestionably permits a more rapid accumulation of individual wealth than with us; but till I had travelled through America, I had no idea how much of the money collected in taxes returns among the people, not only in the purchase of what their industry furnishes, but in the actual enjoyment of what is furnished. Were I an English legislator, instead of sending Sedition to the Tower, I would send her to make a tour of the United States. I had a little leaning towards sedition myself when I set out, but before I had half completed my tour, I was quite cured.

I have read much of the "few and simple wants / of rational man," and I used to I, 62 give a sort of dreamy acquiescence to the reasoning that went to prove each added want an added woe. Those who reason in a comfortable London drawing-room know little about the matter. Were the aliments which sustain life all that we wanted, the faculties of the hog might suffice us; but if we analyze an hour of enjoyment, we shall find that it is made up of agreeable sensations occasioned by a thousand delicate impressions on almost as many nerves; where these nerves are sluggish from never having been awakened, external objects are less important, for they are less perceived; but where the whole machine of the human frame is in full activity, where every sense brings home to consciousness its touch of pleasure or of pain, then every object that meets the senses is important as a vehicle of happiness or misery. But let no frames so tempered visit the United States, or if they do, let it be with no longer pausing than will store the memory with images, which, by the force of contrast, shall sweeten the future.

The "simple" manner of living in West- I, 63 ern / America was more distasteful to me from its levelling effects on the manners of the people, than from the personal privations that it rendered necessary; and yet, till I was without them, I was in no degree aware of the many pleasurable sensations derived from the little elegancies and refinements enjoyed by the middle classes in Europe. There were many circumstances, too trifling even for my gossiping pages, which pressed themselves daily and hourly upon us, and which forced us to remember painfully that we were not at home. It requires an abler pen than mine to trace the connection which I am persuaded exists between these deficiencies and the minds and manners of the people. All animal wants are supplied profusely at Cincinnati, and at a very easy rate; but, alas! these go but a little way in the history of a day's enjoyment. The total and universal want of manners, both in males and females, is so remarkable, that I was constantly endeavouring to account for it. It certainly does not proceed from want of intellect: I have listened to much dull and heavy conversation in America, but rarely to any that I I, 64 could strictly / call silly, (if I except the everywhere privileged class of very young ladies). They appear to me to have clear heads and active intellects; are more ignorant on subjects that are only of conventional value, than on such as are of intrinsic importance; but there is no charm, no grace in their conversation. I very seldom during my whole stay in the country heard a sentence elegantly turned, and correctly pronounced from the lips of an American. There is always something either in the expression or the accent that jars the feelings and shocks the taste.

I will not pretend to decide whether man is better or worse off for requiring refinement in the manners and customs of the society that surrounds him, and for being incapable of enjoyment without them; but in America, that polish which removes the coarser and rougher parts of our nature, is unknown and undreamed of. There is much substantial comfort, and some display in the larger cities; in many of the more obvious features they are as Paris or as London, being all large assemblies of active and intelligent human beings; but yet they are wonderfully unlike in nearly all their / I, 65 moral features. Now God forbid that any reasonable American, (of whom there are so many millions), should ever come to ask me what I mean; I should find it very difficult, nay, perhaps, utterly impossible, to explain myself; but, on the other hand, no European who has visited the Union, will find the least difficulty in understanding me. I am in no way competent to judge of the political institutions of America; and if I should occasionally make an observation on their effects, as they meet my superficial glance, they will be made in the spirit, and with the feeling of a woman, who is apt to tell what her first impressions may be, but unapt to reason back from effects to their causes. Such observations, if they be unworthy of much attention, are also obnoxious to little reproof: but there are points of national peculiarity of which women may judge as ably as men — all that constitutes the external of society may be fairly trusted to us.

Captain Hall, when asked what appeared

to him to constitute the greatest difference between England and America, replied, like a gallant sailor, "the want of loyalty." I, 66 Were the same / question put to me, I should answer, "the want of refinement."

Were Americans, indeed, disposed to assume the plain unpretending deportment of the Switzer, in the days of his picturesque simplicity (when, however, he never chewed tobacco), it would be in bad taste to censure him: but this is not the case; Jonathan will be a fine gentleman, but it must be in his own way. Is he not a freeborn American? Jonathan, however, must remember, that if he will challenge competition with the old world, the old world will now and then look out to see how he supports his pretensions.

With their hours of business, whether judicial or mercantile, civil or military, I have nothing to do; I doubt not they are all spent wisely and profitably; but what are their hours of recreation? Those hours that with us are passed in the enjoyment of all that art can win from nature; when, if the elaborate repast be more deeply relished than sages might approve, it is redeemed from sensuality by the presence of elegance and beauty. What is the American pendant to this? I will not draw any comparisons I, 67 between a good dinner / party in the two countries; I have heard American gentlemen say, that they could perceive no difference between them; but in speaking of general manners, I may observe, that it is rarely they dine in society, except in taverns and boarding-houses. Then they eat with the greatest possible rapidity, and in total silence; I have heard it said by American ladies, that the hours of greatest enjoyment to the gentlemen were those in which a glass of gin cock-tail, or egg-nog, receives its highest relish from the absence of all restraint whatever; and when there were no ladies to trouble them.

Notwithstanding all this, the country is a very fine country, well worth visiting for a thousand reasons; nine hundred and ninety-nine of these are reasons founded on admiration and respect; the thousandth is, that we shall feel the more contented with our own. The more unlike a country through which we travel is to all we have left, the more we are likely to be amused; every thing in Cincinnati had this newness, and I should have thought it a place delightful to visit, but to tarry there was not to feel at home.

My home, however, for a time it was to be. / We heard on every side, that of all I, 68 the known places on "the globe called earth," Cincinnati was the most favourable for a young man to settle in; and I only awaited the arrival of Mr. T. to fix our son there, intending to continue with him till he should feel himself sufficiently established. We accordingly determined upon making ourselves as comfortable as possible. I took a larger house which, however, I did not obtain without considerable difficulty, as, notwithstanding fourteen hundred new dwellings had been erected the preceding year, the demand for houses greatly exceeded the supply. We became acquainted with several amiable people, and we beguiled the anxious interval that preceded Mr. T.'s joining us, by frequent excursions in the neighbourhood, which not only afforded us amusement, but gave us an opportunity of observing the mode of life of the country people.

We visited one farm which interested us particularly from its wild and lonely situation, and from the entire dependence of the inhabitants upon their own resources. It was a partial clearing in the very heart of the forest. The house / was built on the I, 69 side of a hill, so steep that a high ladder was necessary to enter the front door, while the back one opened against the hill side; at the foot of this sudden eminence ran a clear stream, whose bed had been deepened into a little reservoir, just opposite the house. A noble field of Indian corn stretched away into the forest on one side, and a few half-cleared acres, with a shed or two upon them, occupied the other, giving accommodation to cows, horses, pigs, and chickens innumerable. Immediately before the house was a small potatoe-garden, with a few peach and apple trees. The house was built of logs, and consisted of two rooms, besides a little shanty or lean-to, that was used as a kitchen. Both rooms were comfortably furnished with good beds, drawers, &c. The farmer's wife, and a young woman who looked like her sister, were spinning, and three little children were playing about. The woman told me that they spun and wove all the cotton and woollen garments of the family, and knit all the stockings; her husband, though not a shoe-maker by trade, made all the shoes. She manufactured all the soap and candles they used, I, 70 and / prepared her sugar from the sugar-trees on their farm. All she wanted with money, she said, was to buy coffee, tea, and whiskey; and she could "get enough any day by sending a batch of butter and chicken to market." They used no wheat, nor sold any of their corn, which, though it appeared a very large quantity, was not more than they required to make their bread and cakes of various kinds, and to feed all their live stock during the winter. She did not look in health, and said they had all had ague in "the fall;" but she seemed contented, and proud of her independence; though it was in somewhat a mournful accent that she said: " 'Tis strange to see company: I expect the sun may rise and set a hundred times, before I shall see another *human* that does not belong to the family."

I have been minute in the description of this forest-farm, as I think it the best specimen I saw of the back-wood's independence, of which so much is said in America. These people were indeed independent, Robinson Crusoe was hardly more so, and they eat and drink abundantly; but yet it seemed to me that there was something / I, 71 awful and almost unnatural in their loneliness. No village bell ever summoned them to prayer, where they might meet the friendly greeting of their fellow-men. When they die, no spot sacred by ancient reverence will receive their bones — Religion will not breathe her sweet and solemn farewell upon their graves; the husband or the father will dig the pit that is to hold them, beneath the nearest tree; he will himself deposit them within it, and the wind that whispers through the boughs will be their only requiem: but then they pay neither taxes nor tythes, are never expected to pull off a hat or to make a courtesy, and will live and die without hearing or uttering the dreadful words, "God save the king." . . .

Servants — Society — Evening Parties

I, 73 The greatest difficulty in organising a family establishment in Ohio, is getting servants, or, as it is there called, "getting help," for it is more than petty treason to the Republic, to call a free citizen a *servant.* The whole class of young women, whose bread depends upon their labour, are taught to believe that the most abject poverty is preferable to domestic service. Hundreds of half-naked girls work in the paper-mills, or in any other manufactory, for less than half the wages they would receive in service; but they think their equality is compromised by the latter, and nothing but the wish to obtain some particular article of finery will ever induce them to submit to it. A kind friend, however, exerted herself so effectually for me, that a tall stately lass soon presented herself, saying, "I be come to help / I, 74 you." The intelligence was very agreeable, and I welcomed her in the most gracious manner possible, and asked what I should give her by the year.

"Oh Gimini!" exclaimed the damsel, with a loud laugh, "you be a downright Englisher, sure enough. I should like to see a young lady engage by the year in America! I hope I shall get a husband before many months, or I expect I shall be an outright old maid, for I be most seventeen already;

besides, mayhap I may want to go to school. You must just give me a dollar and half a week, and mother's slave, Phillis, must come over once a week, I expect, from t'other side the water, to help me clean."

I agreed to the bargain, of course, with all dutiful submission; and seeing she was preparing to set to work in a yellow dress parsemé with red roses, I gently hinted, that I thought it was a pity to spoil so fine a gown, and that she had better change it.

"'Tis just my best and my worst," she answered; "for I've got no other."

And in truth I found that this young lady I, 75 had / left the paternal mansion with no more clothes of any kind than what she had on. I immediately gave her money to purchase what was necessary for cleanliness and decency, and set to work with my daughters to make her a gown. She grinned applause when our labour was completed; but never uttered the slightest expression of gratitude for that, or for any thing else we could do for her. She was constantly asking us to lend her different articles of dress, and when we declined it, she said, "Well, I never seed such grumpy folks as you be; there is several young ladies of my acquaintance what goes to live out now and then with the old women about the town, and they and their gurls always lends them what they asks for; I guess you Inglish thinks we should poison your things, just as bad as if we was Negurs." And here I beg to assure the reader, that whenever I give conversations they were not made *à loisir,* but were written down immediately after they occurred, with all the verbal fidelity my memory permitted.

This young lady left me at the end of two months; because I refused to lend her I, 76 money / enough to buy a silk dress to go to a ball, saying, "Then 'tis not worth my while to stay any longer."

I cannot imagine it possible that such a state of things can be desirable, or beneficial to any of the parties concerned. I might occupy a hundred pages on the subject, and yet fail to give an adequate idea of the sore, angry, ever-wakeful pride that seemed to torment these poor wretches. In many of them it was so excessive, that all feeling of displeasure, or even of ridicule, was lost in pity. One of these was a pretty girl, whose natural disposition must have been gentle and kind; but her good feelings were soured, and her gentleness turned to morbid sensitiveness, by having heard a thousand and a thousand times that she was as good as any other lady: that all men were equal, and women too; and that it was a sin and a shame for a free-born American to be treated like a servant.

When she found she was to dine in the kitchen, she turned up her pretty lip, and said, "I guess that's 'cause you don't think I'm good enough to eat with you. You'll find that won't do here." I found afterwards that she rarely ate any dinner at / all, I, 77 and generally passed the time in tears. I did every thing in my power to conciliate and make her happy, but I am sure she hated me. I gave her very high wages, and she staid till she had obtained several expensive articles of dress, and then, *un beau matin,* she came to me full dressed, and said, "I must go."—"When shall you return, Charlotte?" — "I expect you'll see no more of me." And so we parted. Her sister was also living with me; but her wardrobe was not yet completed, and she remained some weeks longer, till it was.

I fear it may be called bad taste to say so much concerning my domestics; but, nevertheless, the circumstances are so characteristic of America, that I must recount another history relating to them. A few days after the departure of my ambitious belle, my cries for "Help" had been so effectual, that another young lady presented herself, with the usual preface "I'm come to help you." I had been cautioned never to ask for a reference for character, as it would not only rob me of that help, but entirely prevent my ever getting another; so, five minutes after she entered she was / installed, bundle I, 78 and all, as a member of the family. She was by no means handsome, but there was an air of simple frankness in her manner that won us all. For my own part, I thought I had got a second Jeanie Deans; for she recounted to me histories of her early youth, wherein her plain good sense and strong mind had enabled her to win her way through a host of cruel step-mothers, faithless lovers, and cheating brothers. Among other things, she told me, with the appearance of much emotion, that she had found, since she came to town, a cure for all her sorrows, "Thanks, and praise for it, I have got religion!" and then she asked if I would spare her to go to Meeting every Tuesday and Thursday evening; "You shall not have to want me, Mrs. Trollope; for our minister knows that we have all our duties to perform to man, as well as to God, and he makes the Meeting late in the evening that they may not cross one another." Who could refuse? Not I; and Nancy had leave to go to Meeting two evenings in the week, besides Sundays.

One night, that the mosquitoes had found their way under my net, and prevented my / sleeping, I heard some one enter the house very late; I got up, went to the top of the stairs, and, by the help of a bright moon, recognised Nancy's best bonnet. I called to her. "You are very late," said I; "what is the reason of it?" – "O, Mrs. Trollope," she replied, "I am late, indeed! We have this night had seventeen souls added to our flock. May they live to bless this night! But it has been a long sitting, and very warm; I'll just take a drink of water, and get to bed; you shan't find me later in the morning for it." Nor did I. She was an excellent servant, and performed more than was expected from her; moreover, she always found time to read the Bible several times in the day, and I seldom saw her occupied about any thing without observing that she had placed it near her.

I, 79

At last she fell sick with the cholera, and her life was despaired of. I nursed her with great care, and sat up the greatest part of two nights with her. She was often delirious, and all her wandering thoughts seemed to ramble to heaven. "I have been a sinner," she said, "but I am safe in the Lord Jesus." When she recovered, she asked me to let her go into the country for a few / days, to change the air, and begged me to lend her three dollars.

I, 80

While she was absent a lady called on me, and inquired, with some agitation, if my servant, Nancy Fletcher, were at home. I replied that she was gone into the country. "Thank God," she exclaimed; "never let her enter your doors again, she is the most abandoned woman in the town: a gentleman who knows you, has been told that she lives with you, and that she boasts of having the power of entering your house at any hour of the night." She told many other circumstances, unnecessary to repeat, but all tending to prove that she was a very dangerous inmate.

I expected her home the next evening, and I believe I passed the interval in meditating how to get rid of her without an *éclaircissement*. At length she arrived, and all my study having failed to supply me with any other reason than the real one for dismissing her, I stated it at once. Not the slightest change passed over her countenance, but she looked steadily at me, and said, in a very civil tone, "I should like to know who told you." I replied that it could be of no advantage to her to / know, and that I wished her to go immediately. "I am ready to go," she said, in the same quiet tone; "but what will you do for your three dollars?"—"I must do without them, Nancy; good morning to you." – "I must just put up my things," she said, and left the room. About half an hour afterwards, when we were all assembled at dinner, she entered with her usual civil composed air: "Well, I am come to wish you all good bye," and with a friendly good-humoured smile she left us.

I, 81

This adventure frightened me so heartily, that, notwithstanding I had the dread of cooking my own dinner before my eyes, I would not take any more young ladies into my family without receiving some slight sketch of their former history. At length I met with a very worthy Frenchwoman, and soon after with a tidy English girl, to assist her; and I had the good fortune to keep them till a short time before my departure: so, happily, I have no more misfortunes of this nature to relate.

Such being the difficulties respecting domestic arrangements, it is obvious, that the ladies who are brought up amongst I, 82 them cannot have leisure / for any great development of the mind; it is, in fact, out of the question; and, remembering this, it is more surprising that some among them should be very pleasing, than that none should be highly instructed.

Had I passed as many evenings in company in any other town that I ever visited as I did in Cincinnati, I should have been able to give some little account of the conversations I had listened to; but, upon reading over my notes, and then taxing my memory to the utmost to supply the deficiency, I can scarcely find a trace of any thing that deserves the name. Such as I have, shall be given in their place. But, whatever may be the talents of the persons who meet together in society, the very shape, form, and arrangement of the meeting is sufficient to paralyze conversation. The women invariably herd together at one part of the room, and the men at the other; but, in justice to Cincinnati, I must acknowledge that this arrangement is by no means peculiar to that city, or to the western side of the Alleghanies. Sometimes a small attempt at music produces a partial reunion; a few of the most daring youths, I, 83 animated / by the consciousness of curled hair and smart waistcoats, approach the piano-forte, and begin to mutter a little to the half-grown pretty things, who are comparing with one another "how many quarters' music they have had." Where the mansion is of sufficient dignity to have two drawing-rooms, the piano, the little ladies, and the slender gentlemen are left to themselves, and on such occasions the sound of laughter is often heard to issue from among them. But the fate of the more dignified personages, who are left in the other room, is extremely dismal. The gentlemen spit, talk of elections and the price of produce, and spit again. The ladies look at each other's dresses till they know every pin by heart; talk of Parson Somebody's last sermon on the day of judgment, on Dr. T'otherbody's new pills for dyspepsia, till the "tea" is announced, when they all console themselves together for whatever they may have suffered in keeping awake, by taking more tea, coffee, hot cake and custard, hoe cake, johny cake, waffle cake, and dodger cake, pickled peaches, and preserved cucumbers, ham, turkey, hung beef, apple sauce, and pickled oysters, than ever were prepared / I, 84 in any other country of the known world. After this massive meal is over, they return to the drawing-room, and it always appeared to me that they remained together as long as they could bear it, and then they rise *en masse,* cloak, bonnet, shawl, and exit. . . .

[Art and Lecturers]

I, 89 Cincinnati has not many lions to boast of, but among them / are two museums of natural history; both of these contain many respectable specimens, particularly that of Mr. Dorfeuille, who has, moreover, some highly interesting Indian antiquities. He is a man of taste and science, but a collection formed strictly according to their dictates, would by no means satisfy the western metropolis. The people have a most extravagant passion for wax figures, and the two museums vie with each other in displaying specimens of this barbarous branch of art. As Mr. Dorfeuille cannot trust to his science for attracting the citizens, he has put his ingenuity into requisition, and this has proved to him the surer aid of the two. He has constructed a pandæmonium in an upper story of his museum, in which he has congregated all the images of horror that his fertile fancy could devise; dwarfs that by machinery grow into giants before the eyes of the spectator; imps of ebony with eyes of flame; monstrous reptiles devouring youth and beauty; lakes of fire, and mountains of I, 90 ice; in / short, wax, paint, and springs have done wonders. "To give the scheme some more effect," he makes it visible only through a grate of massive iron bars, among which are arranged wires connected with an electrical machine in a neighbouring chamber; should any daring hand or foot obtrude itself within the bars, it receives a smart shock, that often passes through many of the crowd, and the cause being unknown, the effect is exceedingly comic; terror, astonishment, curiosity, all are set in action, and all contribute to make "Dorfeuille's Hell" one of the most amusing exhibitions imaginable.

There is also a picture gallery at Cincinnati, and this was a circumstance of much interest to us, as our friend Mr. H., who had accompanied Miss Wright to America,[1] in the expectation of finding a good opening in the line of historical painting, intended commencing his experiment at Cincinnati. It would be invidious to describe the picture gallery; I have no doubt, that some years hence it will present a very different appearance. Mr. H. was very kindly received by many of the gentlemen of the city, and though the state of the fine I, 91 arts / there gave him but little hope that he should meet with much success, he immediately occupied himself in painting a noble historical picture of the landing of General Lafayette at Cincinnati.

Perhaps the clearest proof of the little feeling for art that existed at that time in Cincinnati, may be drawn from the result of an experiment originated by a German, who taught drawing there. He conceived the project of forming a chartered academy of fine arts; and he succeeded in the beginning to his utmost wish, or rather, "they fooled him to the top of his bent." Three thousand dollars were subscribed, that is to say, names were written against different sums to that amount, a house was chosen, and finally, application was made to the government, and the charter obtained, rehearsing formally the names of the subscribing members, the professors, and the officers. So far did the steam of their zeal impel them, but at this point it was let off; the affair stood still, and I never heard the academy of fine arts mentioned afterwards.

This same German gentleman, on seeing Mr. H.'s sketches, was so well pleased with them, that / he immediately proposed his I, 92 joining him in his drawing school, with an agreement, I believe, that his payment from it should be five hundred dollars a year. Mr. H. accepted the proposal; but the union did not last long, and the cause of its dissolution was too American to be omitted. Mr. H. prepared his models, and attended the class, which was numerous, consisting both of boys and girls. He soon found that the "sage called Decipline" was not one of the assistants, and he remonstrated against the constant talking, and running from one part of the room to another, but in vain; finding, however, that he could do nothing till this was discontinued, he wrote some rules, enforcing order, for the purpose of placing them at the door of the academy. When he showed them to his colleague, he shook his head, and said; "Very goot, very goot in Europe, but America boys and gals vill not bear it, dey will do just vat dey please; Suur, dey vould all go avay next day." "And you will not enforce these regulations *si nécessaires,* Monsieur?" "O lar! not for de vorld." "*Eh bien,* Monsieur, I must leave the young republicans to your management."

I heard another anecdote that will help I, 93 to show the state of art at this time in the west. Mr. Bullock was showing to some gentlemen of the first standing, the very *élite* of Cincinnati, his beautiful collection of engravings, when one among them exclaimed, "Have you really done all these since you came here? How hard you must have worked!"

I was also told of a gentleman of High Cincinnati *ton,* and critical in his taste for

[1] Frances Wright was a Scottish freethinker and feminist who took up residence in the United States in 1824 and who worked for gradual emancipation of the slave, recognition of labor, and advancement of public education.

the fine arts, who, having a drawing put into his hands, representing Hebe and the bird, umquhile sacred to Jupiter, demanded in a satirical tone, "What is this?" "Hebe," replied the alarmed collector. "Hebe," sneered the man of taste, "What the devil has Hebe to do with the American eagle?"

We had not been long at Cincinnati when Dr. Caldwell, the Spurzheim of America, arrived there, for the purpose of delivering lectures on phrenology. I attended his lectures, and was introduced to him. He has studied Spurzheim and Combe diligently, and seems to understand the science to which he has devoted himself; but neither his lectures nor his conversation had that / delightful truth of genuine enthusiasm, which makes listening to Dr. Spurzheim so great a treat. His lectures, however, produced considerable effect. Between twenty and thirty of the most erudite citizens decided upon forming a phrenological society. A meeting was called, and fully attended; a respectable number of subscribers' names was registered, the payment of subscriptions being arranged for a future day. President, vice-president, treasurer, and secretary, were chosen; and the first meeting dissolved with every appearance of energetic perseverance in scientific research.

I, 94

The second meeting brought together one-half of this learned body, and they enacted rules and laws, and passed resolutions, sufficient, it was said, to have filled three folios.

A third day of meeting arrived, which was an important one, as on this occasion the subscriptions were to be paid. The treasurer came punctually, but found himself alone. With patient hope, he waited two hours for the wise men of the west, but he waited in vain: and so expired the Phrenological Society of Cincinnati.

I, 95

I had often occasion to remark that the spirit of enterprise or improvement seldom glowed with sufficient ardour to resist the smothering effect of a demand for dollars. The Americans love talking. All great works, however, that promise a profitable result, are sure to meet support from men who have enterprise and capital sufficient to await the return; but where there is nothing but glory, or the gratification of taste to be expected, it is, I believe, very rarely that they give any thing beyond "their most sweet voices."

Perhaps they are right. In Europe we see fortunes crippled by a passion for statues, or for pictures, or for books, or for gems; for all and every of the artificial wants that give grace to life, and tend to make man forget that he is a thing of clay. They are wiser in their generation on the other side of the Atlantic; I rarely saw any thing that led to such oblivion there.

Soon after Dr. Caldwell's departure, another lecturer appeared upon the scene, whose purpose of publicly addressing the people was no sooner made known, than the most violent sensation was excited.

I, 96

That a lady of fortune, family, and education, whose youth had been passed in the most refined circles of private life, should present herself to the people as a public lecturer, would naturally excite surprise any where, and the *nil admirari* of the old world itself, would hardly be sustained before such a spectacle; but in America, where women are guarded by a seven-fold shield of habitual insignificance, it caused an effect that can hardly be described. "Miss Wright, of Nashoba, is going to lecture at the court-house" sounded from street to street, and from house to house. I shared the surprise, but not the wonder; I knew her extraordinary gift of eloquence, her almost unequalled command of words, and the wonderful power of her rich and thrilling voice; and I doubted not that if it was her will to do it, she had the power of commanding the attention, and enchanting the ear of any audience before whom it was her pleasure to appear. I was most anxious to hear her, but was almost deterred from attempting it, by the reports that reached me of the immense crowd that was expected. After many consultations, and hearing that many other ladies / intended going, my friend Mrs. P****, and myself, decided

I, 97

upon making the attempt, accompanied by a party of gentlemen, and found the difficulty less than we anticipated, though the building was crowded in every part. We congratulated ourselves that we had had the courage to be among the number, for all my expectations fell far short of the splendour, the brilliance, the overwhelming eloquence of this extraordinary orator.

Her lecture was upon the nature of true knowledge, and it contained little that could be objected to, by any sect or party; it was intended as an introduction to the strange and startling theories contained in her subsequent lectures, and could alarm only by the hints it contained that the fabric of human wisdom could rest securely on no other base than that of human knowledge.

There was, however, one passage from which common-sense revolted; it was one wherein she quoted that phrase of mischievous sophistry, "all men are born free and equal."

This false and futile axiom, which has done, is doing, and will do so much harm to this fine / country, came from Jefferson; I, 98 and truly his life was a glorious commentary upon it. I pretend not to criticise his written works, but common-sense enables me to pronounce this, his favourite maxim, false. . . .

Removal to the Country

I, 139 The extraordinary familiarity of our poor neighbours [Mrs. Trollope was now living a mile and a half from Cincinnati.] startled us at first, and we hardly knew how to receive their uncouth advances, or what was expected of us in return; however, it sometimes produced very laughable scenes. Upon one occasion, two of my children set off upon an exploring walk up the hills; they were absent rather longer than we expected, and the rest of our party determined upon going out to meet them; we knew the direction they had taken, but thought it would be as well to inquire at a little public-house at the bottom of the hill, if such a pair had been seen to pass. A woman, whose appearance more resembled a Covent Garden market-woman than any thing else I can remember, came out and answered my question with the most jovial good humour in the affirmative, and prepared to join us in our search. Her look, her voice, her manner, were so exceedingly coarse and vehement, that she almost frightened me; she passed her arm within mine, and to the inexpressible amusement of my young people, she dragged me on, talking and questioning me without ceasing. She lived but a short distance from us, and I am sure intended to be a very good neighbour; but her / violent intimacy made me I, 140 dread to pass her door; my children, including my sons, she always addressed by their Christian names, excepting when she substituted the word "honey;" this familiarity of address, however, I afterwards found was universal throughout all ranks in the United States.

My general appellation amongst my neighbours was "the English old woman," but in mentioning each other they constantly employed the term "lady;" and they evidently had a pleasure in using it, for I repeatedly observed, that in speaking of a neighbour, instead of saying Mrs. Such-a-one, they described her as "the lady over the way what takes in washing," or as "that there lady, out by the Gulley, what is making dip-candles." Mr. Trollope was as constantly called "the old man," while draymen, butchers' boys, and the labourers on the canal, were invariably denominated "them gentlemen;" nay, we once saw one of the most gentleman-like men in Cincinnati introduce a fellow in dirty shirt-sleeves, and all sorts of detestable et cetera, to one of his friends, with this formula, "D***** let me introduce this gentleman to you."

I, 141 Our respective titles certainly were not very important; but the eternal shaking hands with these ladies and gentlemen was really an annoyance, and the more so, as the near approach of the gentlemen was always redolent of whiskey and tobacco.

But the point where this republican equality was the most distressing was in the long and frequent visitations that it produced. No one dreams of fastening a door in Western America; I was told that it would be considered as an affront by the whole neighbourhood. I was thus exposed to perpetual, and most vexatious interruptions from people whom I had often never seen, and whose names still oftener were unknown to me.

Those who are native there, and to the manner born, seem to pass over these annoyances with more skill than I could ever acquire. More than once I have seen some of my acquaintance beset in the same way, without appearing at all distressed by it; they continued their employment or conversation with me, much as if no such interruption had taken place; when the visitor / entered, they would say, "How do you do?" and shake hands.

I, 142

"Tolerable, I thank ye; how be you?" was the reply.

If it was a female, she took off her hat; if a male, he kept it on, and then taking possession of the first chair in their way, they would retain it for an hour together, without uttering another word; at length, rising abruptly, they would again shake hands, with, "Well, now I must be going, I guess," and so take themselves off, apparently well contented with their reception.

I could never attain this philosophical composure; I could neither write nor read, and I always fancied I must talk to them. I will give the minutes of a conversation which I once set down after one of their visits, as a specimen of their tone and manner of speaking and thinking. My visitor was a milkman.

"Well now, so you be from the old country? Ay – you'll see sights here, I guess."

"I hope I shall see many."

I, 143

"That's a fact. I expect your little place of an island don't grow such dreadful fine corn as you sees here?"

"It grows no corn at all, sir."

"Possible! no wonder, then, that we reads such awful stories in the papers of your poor people being starved to death."

"We have wheat, however."

"Ay, for your rich folks, but I calculate the poor seldom gets a belly full."

"You have certainly much greater abundance here."

"I expect so. Why they do say, that if a poor body contrives to be smart enough to scrape together a few dollars, that your King George always comes down upon 'em, and takes it all away. Don't he?"

"I do not remember hearing of such a transaction."

"I guess they be pretty close about it. Your papers ben't like ourn, I reckon? Now we says and prints just what we likes."

"You spend a good deal of time in reading the newspapers."

"And I'd like you to tell me how we can spend / it better. How should freemen spend their time, but looking after their government, and watching that them fellers as we gives offices to, doos their duty, and gives themselves no airs?"

I, 144

"But I sometimes think, sir, that your fences might be in more thorough repair, and your roads in better order, if less time was spent in politics."

"The Lord! to see how little you knows of a free country! Why, what's the smoothness of a road, put against the freedom of a free-born American? And what does a broken zig zag signify, comparable to knowing that the men what we have been pleased to send up to Congress, speaks handsome and straight, as we chooses they should?"

"It is from a sense of duty, then, that you all go to the liquor store to read the papers?"

"To be sure it is, and he'd be no true-born American as didn't. I don't say that the father of a family should always be after liquor, but I do say that I'd rather have my son drunk three times in a week, than not look after the affairs of his country." . . .

[Life in Mohawk, Ohio]

I, 163 Mohawk, as our little village was called, gave us an excellent opportunity of comparing the peasants of the United States with those of England, and of judging the average degree of comfort enjoyed by each. I believe Ohio gives as fair a specimen as any part of the Union; if they have the roughness and inconveniences of a new state to contend with, they have higher wages and cheaper provisions; if I err in supposing it a mean state in point of comfort, it certainly is not in taking too low a standard.

Mechanics, if good workmen, are certain of employment and good wages, rather higher than with us; the average wages of a labourer throughout the Union is ten dollars a month, with / lodging, boarding, washing, and mending; if he lives at his own expense he has a dollar a day. It appears to me that the necessaries of life, that is to say, meat, bread, butter, tea, and coffee, (not to mention whiskey), are within the reach of every sober, industrious, and healthy man who chooses to have them; and yet I think that an English peasant, with the same qualifications, would, in coming to the United States, change for the worse. He would find wages somewhat higher, and provisions in Western America considerably lower; but this statement, true as it is, can lead to nothing but delusion if taken apart from other facts, fully as certain, and not less important, but which require more detail in describing, and which perhaps cannot be fully comprehended, except by an eye-witness. The American poor are accustomed to eat meat three times a day; I never inquired into the habits of any cottagers in Western America where this was not the case. I found afterwards in Maryland, Pennsylvania, and other parts of the country, where the price of meat was higher, that it was used with more economy; yet still a much larger portion of the weekly income is thus / expended than with us. Ardent spirits, though lamentably cheap, still cost something, and the use of them among the men, with more or less of discretion, according to the character, is universal. Tobacco also grows at their doors, and is not taxed; yet this too costs something, and the air of heaven is not in more general use among the men of America, than chewing tobacco. I am not now pointing out the evils of dram-drinking; but it is evident, that where this practice prevails universally, and often to the most frightful excess, the consequence must be, that the money spent to obtain the dram is less than the money lost by the time consumed in drinking it. Long, disabling, and expensive fits of sickness are incontestably more frequent in every part of America, than in England, and the sufferers have no aid to look to, but what they have saved, or what they may be enabled to sell. I have never seen misery exceed what I have witnessed in an American cottage where disease had entered.

But if the condition of the labourer be not superior to that of the English peasant, that of his wife and daughters is incomparably worse. It is they who are indeed the slaves of the soil. One has but to look at the wife of an American cottager, and ask her age, to be convinced that the life she leads is one of hardship, privation, and labour. It is rare to see a woman in this station who has reached the age of thirty, without losing every trace of youth and beauty. You continually see women with infants on their knee, that you feel sure are their grand-children, till some convincing proof of the contrary is displayed. Even the young girls, though often with lovely features, look pale, thin, and haggard. I do not remember to have seen in any single instance among the poor, a specimen of the plump, rosy, laughing physiognomy so common among our cottage girls. The horror of domestic service, which the reality of slavery, and the fable of equality, have generated, excludes the young women from that sure and most comfortable resource of decent English girls; and the consequence is, that with a most irreverend freedom of manner to the parents, the /

daughters are, to the full extent of the word, domestic slaves. This condition, which no periodical merry-making, no village *fête,* ever occurs to cheer, is only changed for the still sadder burdens of a teeming wife. They marry very young; in fact, in no rank of life do you meet with young women in that delightful period of existence between childhood and marriage, wherein, if only tolerably well spent, so much useful information is gained, and the character takes a sufficient degree of firmness to support with dignity the more important parts of wife and mother. The slender, childish thing, without vigour of mind or body, is made to stem a sea of troubles that dims her young eye and makes her cheek grow pale, even before nature has given it the last beautiful finish of the full-grown woman.

"We shall get along," is the answer in full, for all that can be said in way of advice to a boy and girl, who take it into their heads to go before a magistrate and "get married." And they do get along, till sickness overtakes them, by means perhaps of borrowing a kettle from one and a tea-pot from another; but intemperance, idleness, or sickness / will, in one week, plunge those who are even getting along well, into utter destitution; and where this happens, they are completely without resource.

I, 168

The absence of poor-laws is, without doubt, a blessing to the country, but they have not that natural and reasonable dependence on the richer classes which, in countries differently constituted, may so well supply their place. I suppose there is less alms-giving in America than in any other Christian country on the face of the globe. It is not in the temper of the people either to give or to receive.

I extract the following pompous passage from a Washington paper of Feb. 1829, (a season of uncommon severity and distress), which, I think, justifies my observation.

"Among the liberal evidences of sympathy for the suffering poor of this city, two have come to our knowledge which deserve to be especially noticed: the one a donation by the President of the United States to the committee of the ward in which he resides of fifty dollars; the other the donation by a few of the officers of the war / department to the Howard and Dorcas Societies, of seventy-two dollars." When such mention is made of a gift of about nine pounds sterling from the sovereign magistrate of the United States, and of thirteen pounds sterling as a contribution from one of the state departments, the inference is pretty obvious, that the sufferings of the destitute in America are not liberally relieved by individual charity.

I, 169

I had not been three days at Mohawk Cottage before a pair of ragged children came to ask for medicine for a sick mother; and when it was given to them, the eldest produced a handful of cents, and desired to know what he was to pay. The superfluous milk of our cow was sought after eagerly, but every new-comer always proposed to pay for it. When they found out that "the English old woman" did not sell any thing, I am persuaded they by no means liked her the better for it; but they seemed to think, that if she were a fool it was no reason they should be so too, and accordingly the borrowing, as they called it, became very constant, but always in a form that showed their dignity and freedom. One woman sent to / borrow a pound of cheese; another half a pound of coffee; and more than once an intimation accompanied the milk-jug, that the milk must be fresh, and unskimmed: on one occasion the messenger refused milk, and said "Mother only wanted a little cream for her coffee."

I, 170

I could never teach them to believe, during above a year that I lived at this house, that I would not sell the old clothes of the family; and so pertinacious were they in bargain-making, that often, when I had given them the articles which they wanted to purchase, they would say, "Well, I expect I shall have to do a turn of work for this; you may send for me when you want me." But as I never did ask for the turn of work, and as this formula was constantly repeated, I began to suspect that it was spoken solely to avoid uttering that most un-American phrase, "I thank you."

There was one man whose progress in wealth I watched with much interest and pleasure. When I first became his neighbour, himself, his wife, and four children, were living in one room, with plenty of I, 171 beef-steaks and onions for / breakfast, dinner, and supper; but with very few other comforts. He was one of the finest men I ever saw, full of natural intelligence and activity of mind and body, but he could neither read nor write. He drank but little whiskey, and but rarely chewed tobacco, and was therefore more free from that plague-spot of spitting, which rendered male colloquy so difficult to endure. He worked for us frequently, and often used to walk into the drawing-room and seat himself on the sofa, and tell me all his plans. He made an engagement with the proprietor of the wooded hill before mentioned, by which half the wood he could fell was to be his own. His unwearied industry made this a profitable bargain, and from the proceeds he purchased the materials for building a comfortable frame (or wooden) house; he did the work almost entirely himself. He then got a job for cutting rails; and as he could cut twice as many in a day as any other man in the neighbourhood, he made a good thing of it. He then let half his pretty house, which was admirably constructed, with an ample portico, that kept it always cool. His next step was contract- I, 172 ing for the building a wooden / bridge; and when I left Mohawk, he had fitted up his half of the building as an hotel and grocery store; and I have no doubt that every sun that sets sees him a richer man than when it rose. He hopes to make his son a lawyer; and I have little doubt that he will live to see him sit in Congress; when this time arrives, the wood-cutter's son will rank with any other member of Congress, not of courtesy, but of right; and the idea that his origin is a disadvantage, will never occur to the imagination of the most exalted of his fellow-citizens.

This is the only feature in American society that I recognise as indicative of the equality they profess. Any man's son may become the equal of any other man's son; and the consciousness of this is certainly a spur to exertion: on the other hand, it is also a spur to that coarse familiarity, untempered by any shadow of respect, which is assumed by the grossest and the lowest in their intercourse with the highest and most refined. This is a positive evil; and, I think, more than balances its advantages.

And here again it may be observed, that the theory of equality may be very daintily discussed / by English gentlemen in a I, 173 London dining-room, when the servant, having placed a fresh bottle of cool wine on the table, respectfully shuts the door, and leaves them to their walnuts and their wisdom; but it will be found less palatable when it presents itself in the shape of a hard, greasy paw, and is claimed in accents that breathe less of freedom than of onions and whiskey. Strong, indeed, must be the love of equality in an English breast, if it can survive a tour through the Union. . . .

Theatre — Delicacy — Visit of the President

I, 183 The theatre at Cincinnati is small, and not very brilliant in decoration, but in the absence of every other amusement our young men frequently attended it, and in the bright clear nights of autumn and winter, the mile and a half of distance was not enough to prevent the less enterprising members of the family from sometimes accompanying them. The great inducement to this was the excellent acting of Mr. and Mrs. Alexander Drake, the managers.[1] . . .

The theatre was really not a bad one, I, 187 though the very poor receipts rendered it impossible to keep it in high order; but an annoyance infinitely greater than decorations indifferently clean, was the style and

[1] The Drakes were English.

manner of the audience. Men came into the lower tier of boxes without their coats; and I have seen shirt sleeves tucked up to the shoulder; the spitting was incessant, and the mixed smell of onions and whiskey was enough to make one feel even the Drakes' acting dearly bought by the obligation of enduring its accompaniments. The bearing and attitudes of the men are perfectly indescribable; the heels thrown higher than the head, the entire rear of the person presented to the audience, the whole length supported on the benches, are among the varieties that these exquisite posture-masters exhibit. The noises, too, were perpetual, and of the most unpleasant kind; the applause is expressed by cries and thumping with the feet, instead of clapping; / [I, 188] and when a patriotic fit seized them, and "Yankee Doodle" was called for, every man seemed to think his reputation as a citizen depended on the noise he made.

Two very indifferent figurantes, probably from the Ambigu Comique, or la Gaieté, made their appearance at Cincinnati while we were there; and had Mercury stepped down, and danced a *pas seul* upon earth, his godship could not have produced a more violent sensation. But wonder and admiration were by no means the only feelings excited; horror and dismay were produced in at least an equal degree. No one, I believe, doubted their being admirable dancers, but every one agreed that the morals of the Western world would never recover the shock. When I was asked if I had ever seen any thing so dreadful before, I was embarrassed how to answer; for the young women had been exceedingly careful, both in their dress and in their dancing, to meet the taste of the people; but had it been Virginie in her most transparent attire, or Taglioni in her most remarkable pirouette, they could not have been more reprobated. The ladies altogether forsook the theatre; the / [I, 189] gentlemen muttered under their breath, and turned their heads aside when the subject was mentioned; the clergy denounced them from the pulpit; and if they were named at the meetings of the saints, it was to show how deep the horror such a theme could produce. I could not but ask myself if virtue were a plant, thriving under one form in one country, and flourishing under a different one in another? If these Western Americans are right, then how dreadfully wrong are we! It is really a very puzzling subject.

But this was not the only point on which I found my notions of right and wrong utterly confounded; hardly a day passed in which I did not discover that something or other that I had been taught to consider lawful as eating, was held in abhorrence by those around me; many words to which I had never heard an objectionable meaning attached were totally interdicted, and the strangest paraphrastic sentences substituted. I confess it struck me, that notwithstanding a general stiffness of manner, which I think must exceed that of the Scribes and Pharisees, the Americans have imaginations that kindle with alarming facility. / [I, 190] I could give many anecdotes to prove this, but will content myself with a few.

A young German gentleman of perfectly good manners, once came to me greatly chagrined at having offended one of the principal families in the neighbourhood, by having pronounced the word *corset* before the ladies of it. An old female friend had kindly overcome her own feelings so far as to mention to him the cause of the coolness he had remarked, and strongly advised his making an apology. He told me that he was perfectly well disposed to do so, but felt himself greatly at a loss how to word it. . . .

[I, 191] At Cincinnati there is a garden where the people go to eat ices, and to look at roses. For the preservation of the flowers, there is placed at the end of one of the walks a sign-post sort of daub, representing a Swiss peasant girl, holding in her hand a scroll, requesting that the roses might not be gathered. Unhappily for the artist, or for the proprietor, or for both, the petticoat of this figure was so short as to show her ancles. The ladies saw, and shuddered; and it was formally intimated to the proprietor, that if he wished for the patronage of the ladies of Cincinnati, he must have the petticoat of this figure lengthened. The affrighted purveyor of ices sent off an express for the artist and his paint pot. He came, but unluckily not provided with any colour that would match the petticoat; the necessity, however, was / too urgent for delay, and a flounce of blue was added to the petticoat of red, giving bright and shining evidence before all men, of the immaculate delicacy of the Cincinnati ladies. . . . (I, 192)

(I, 196) And now the time arrived that our domestic circle was again to be broken up. Our eldest son was to be entered at Oxford, and it was necessary that his father should accompany him: and, after considerable indecision, it was at length determined that I and my / daughters should remain another year with our second son. (I, 197) It was early in February, and our travellers prepared themselves to encounter some sharp gales upon the mountains, though the great severity of the cold appeared to be past. We got buffalo robes and double shoes prepared for them, and they were on the eve of departure when we heard that General Jackson, the newly-elected President, was expected to arrive immediately at Cincinnati, from his residence in the West, and to proceed by steam-boat to Pittsburgh, on his way to Washington. This determined them not to fix the day of their departure till they heard of his arrival, and / then, if possible, to start in the same boat with him; (I, 198) the decent dignity of a private conveyance not being deemed necessary for the President of the United States.

The day of his arrival was however quite uncertain, and we could only determine to have every thing very perfectly in readiness, let it come when it would. This resolution was hardly acted upon when the news reached us that the General had arrived at Louisville, and was expected at Cincinnati in a few hours. All was bustle and hurry at Mohawk Cottage; we quickly dispatched our packing business, and this being the first opportunity we had had of witnessing such a demonstration of popular feeling, we all determined to be present at the debarkation of the great man. We accordingly walked to Cincinnati, and secured a favourable station at the landing-place, both for the purpose of seeing the first magistrate, and of observing his reception by the people. We had waited but a few moments when the heavy panting of the steam-engines and then a discharge of cannon told that we were just in time; another moment brought his vessel in sight.

(I, 199) Nothing could be better of its kind than his approach to the shore: the noble steamboat which conveyed him was flanked on each side by one of nearly equal size and splendour; the roofs of all three were covered by a crowd of men; cannon saluted them from the shore as they passed by, to the distance of a quarter of a mile above the town, there they turned about, and came down the river with a rapid but stately motion, the three vessels so close together as to appear one mighty mass upon the water.

When they arrived opposite the principal landing, they swept gracefully round, and the side vessels, separating themselves from the centre, fell a few feet back, permitting her to approach before them with her honoured freight. All this manœuvring was extremely well executed, and really beautiful.

The crowd on the shore awaited her arrival in perfect stillness. When she touched the bank the people on board gave a faint huzza, but it was answered by no note of welcome from the land: this cold silence was certainly not produced by any want of friendly feeling towards the new / President; (I, 200) during the whole of the canvassing he had been decidedly the popular candidate at Cincinnati, and for months past, we had been accustomed to the cry of "Jackson for ever" from an overwhelming majority; but enthusiasm is not either the virtue or the vice of America.

More than one private carriage was stationed at the water's edge to await the General's orders, but they were dismissed with the information that he would walk to the hotel. Upon receiving this intimation the silent crowd divided itself in a very orderly manner, leaving a space for him to walk through them. He did so, uncovered, though the distance was considerable, and the weather very cold; but he alone (with the exception of a few European gentlemen who were present) was without a hat. He wore his grey hair, carelessly, but not ungracefully arranged, and, spite of his harsh gaunt features, he looks like a gentleman and a soldier. He was in deep mourning, having very recently lost his wife; they were said to have been very happy together, and I was pained by hearing a voice near me exclaim, as he approached the spot where I I, 201 stood, "There goes Jackson, where / is his wife?" Another sharp voice, at a little distance, cried: "Adams for ever!" And these sounds were all I heard to break the silence.

"They manage these matters better" in the East, I have no doubt, but as yet I was still in the West, and still inclined to think that, however meritorious the American character may be, it is not amiable.

Mr. T. and his sons joined the group of citizens who waited upon him to the hotel, and were presented to the President in form; that is, they shook hands with him. Learning that he intended to remain a few hours there, or more properly, that it would be a few hours before the steam-boat would be ready to proceed, Mr. T. secured berths on board, and returned, to take a hasty dinner with us. At the hour appointed by the captain, Mr. T. and his son accompanied the General on board, and by subsequent letters I learnt that they had conversed a good deal with him, and were pleased by his conversation and manners, but deeply disgusted by the brutal familiarity to which they saw him exposed at every place on their progress at which they stopped; I am tempted to quote one passage, as sufficiently / descriptive of the manner, which I, 202 so painfully grated against their European feelings.

"There was not a hulking boy from a keel-boat who was not introduced to the President, unless, indeed, as was the case with some, they introduced themselves; for instance, I was at his elbow when a greasy fellow accosted him thus: –

" 'General Jackson, I guess?'

"The General bowed assent.

" 'Why they told me you was dead.'

" 'No! Providence has hitherto preserved my life.'

" 'And is your wife alive too?'

"The General, apparently much hurt, signified the contrary, upon which the courtier concluded his harangue by saying, 'Ay, I thought it was the one or the t'other of ye.' " . . .

Departure from Cincinnati

I, 255 We quitted Cincinnati the beginning of March, 1830, and I believe there was not one of our party who did not experience a sensation of pleasure in leaving it. We had seen again and again all the queer varieties of its little world; had amused ourselves with its consequence, its taste, and its *ton,* till they had ceased to be amusing. Not a hill was left unclimbed, nor a forest path unexplored; and, with the exception of two or three individuals, who bore heads and hearts peculiar to no clime, but which are found scattered through the world, as if to keep us every where in good humour with it, we left nought to regret at Cincinnati. The only regret was, that we had ever entered it; for we had wasted health, time, and money there.

We got on board the steam-boat which was to convey us to Wheeling at three o'clock. She was a noble boat, by far the finest we had seen. . . .

I, 258 The separation of the sexes, so often mentioned, is no where more remarkable than on board the steam-boats. Among the passengers on this occasion we had a gentleman and his wife, who really appeared to suffer from the arrangement. She was an invalid, and he was extremely attentive to her, as far, at least, as the regulations permitted. When the steward opened the door of communication between the cabins, to permit our approaching the table, her husband was always stationed close to it, to hand her to her place; and when he accompanied her again to the door, he always lingered for a moment or two on the forbidden threshold, nor left his station, till the last female had passed through. Once or twice he ventured, when all but his wife were on the balcony, to sit down beside her for a moment in our cabin, but the instant either of us entered, he started like a guilty thing and vanished.

While mentioning the peculiar arrangements which are thought necessary to the delicacy of the American ladies, or to the comfort of the American gentlemen, I am tempted to allude to a story which I saw in the papers respecting the visits which it was stated Captain Basil Hall persisted in I, 259 making / to his wife and child on board a Mississippi steam-boat, after being informed that doing so was contrary to law. Now I happen to know that neither himself or Mrs. Hall ever entered the ladies' cabin during the whole voyage, as they occupied a state-room which Captain Hall had secured for his party. The veracity of newspaper statements is, perhaps, nowhere quite unimpeachable, but if I am not greatly mistaken, there are more direct falsehoods circulated by the American newspapers than by all the others in the world, and the one great and never-failing source of these voluminous works of imagination is England and the English. How differently would such a voyage as we were now making be managed on the other side the Atlantic, were such a mode of travelling possible there. Such long calm river excursions would be perfectly delightful, and parties would be perpetually formed to enjoy them. Even were all the parties strangers to each other, the knowledge that they were to eat, drink, and steam away together for a week or fortnight, would induce something like a social feeling in any other country.

It is true that the men became sufficiently acquainted / to game together, and we were I, 260 told that the opportunity was considered as so favourable, that no boat left New Orleans without having as cabin passengers one or two gentlemen from that city whose profession it was to drill the fifty-two elements of a pack of cards to profitable duty. This doubtless is an additional reason for the strict exclusion of the ladies from their society. The constant drinking of spirits is another; for though they do not scruple to chew tobacco and to spit incessantly in the presence of women, they generally prefer drinking and gaming in their absence.

I often used to amuse myself with fancying the different scene which such a vessel would display in Europe. The noble length of the gentlemen's cabin would be put into requisition for a dance, while that of the ladies', with their delicious balcony, would be employed for refreshments, instead of sitting down in two long silent melancholy rows, to swallow as much coffee and beefsteak as could be achieved in ten minutes. Then song and music would be heard borne along by the midnight breeze; but on the Ohio, when light failed to show us the bluffs, and the trees, with their images inverted in the stream, we crept into our little cots, listening to the ceaseless churning of the engine, in hope it would prove a lullaby till morning. . . .

American Beauty — Gallery of Fine Arts — Antiques

II, 81 One evening, while the rest of my party went to visit some objects which I had before seen, I agreed to await their return in this square, [Washington Square in Philadelphia] and sat down under a magnificent catalpa, which threw its fragrant blossoms in all directions; the other end of the bench was occupied by a young lady who was employed in watching the gambols of a little boy. There was something in her manner of looking at me and exchanging a smile when her young charge performed some extraordinary feat of activity on the grass, that persuaded me she was not an American. I do not remember who spoke first, but we were presently in a full flow II, 82 of conversation. She spoke English with / elegant correctness, but she was a German, and with an ardour of feeling which gave her a decidedly foreign air in Philadelphia, she talked to me of her country, of all she had left, and of all she had found, or rather of all she had not found, for thus ran her lament: —

"They do not love music, Oh no! and they never amuse themselves — no; and their hearts are not warm, at least they seem not so to strangers; and they have no ease, no forgetfulness of business and of care — no, not for a moment. But I will not stay long, I think, for I should not live."

She told me that she had a brother settled there as a merchant, and that she had passed a year with him; but she was hoping soon to return to her father-land.

I never so strongly felt the truth of the remark that expression is the soul of beauty, as in looking at, and listening to this young German. She was any thing but handsome; it is true she had large eyes, full of gentle expression, but every feature was irregular; but, oh! the charm of that smile, of that look of deep feeling which animated every feature when she spoke of her own Ger- II, 83 many! The tone of / her voice, the slight and graceful action which accompanied her words, all struck me as so attractive, that the half hour I passed with her was continually recurring to my memory. I had often taxed myself with feeling something like prejudice against the beautiful American women; but this half hour set my conscience at rest; it is not prejudice which causes one to feel that regularity of features is insufficient to interest, or even to please, beyond the first glance. I certainly believe the women of America to be the handsomest in the world, but as surely do I believe that they are the least attractive.

We visited the nineteenth annual exhibition of the Pennsylvanian academy of the fine arts; 431 was the number of objects exhibited, which were so arranged as to fill three tolerably large rooms, and one smaller, called the director's room. There were among the number about thirty engravings, and a much larger proportion of water-colour drawings, about seventy had the P. A. (Pennsylvanian Academician) annexed to the name of the artist.

II, 84 The principal historical composition was a large scripture piece by Mr. Washington Alston. This gentleman is spoken of as an artist of great merit, and I was told that his manner was much improved since this picture was painted (it bears date, 1813). I believe it was for this picture Mr. Alston received a prize at the British Gallery.

There was a portrait of a lady, which in the catalogue is designated as "the White Plume," which had the reputation of being the most admired in the collection, and the artist, Mr. Ingham, is said to rank highest among the portrait-painters of America. This picture is of very high finish, particularly the drapery, which is most elaborately worked, even to the pile of the velvet; the management of the light is much in the manner of Good; but the drawing is very defective, and the contour, though the face is a lovely one, hard and unfleshy. From all the conversations on painting, which I listened to in America, I found that the finish of drapery was considered as the highest excellence, and next to this, the resemblance in a portrait; I do not remember ever to have heard / the words *drawing* or *composition* used in any conversation on the II, 85 subject.

One of the rooms of this academy has inscribed over its door

ANTIQUE STATUE GALLERY

The door was open, but just within it was a screen, which prevented any objects in the room being seen from without. Upon my pausing to read this inscription, an old woman who appeared to officiate as guardian of the gallery, bustled up, and addressing me with an air of much mystery, said, "Now ma'am, now; this is just the time for you — nobody can see you — make haste."

I stared at her with unfeigned surprise, and disengaging my arm, which she had taken apparently to hasten my movements, I very gravely asked her meaning.

"Only, ma'am, that the ladies like to go into that room by themselves, when there be no gentlemen watching them."

On entering this mysterious apartment, the first thing I remarked, was a written paper, deprecating / the disgusting depravity which had led some of the visitors to mark and deface the casts in a most indecent and shameless manner. This abomination has unquestionably been occasioned by the coarse-minded custom which sends alternate groups of males and females into the room. Were the antique gallery thrown open to mixed parties of ladies and gentlemen, it would soon cease. Till America has reached the degree of refinement which permits of this, the antique casts should not be exhibited to ladies at all. I never felt my delicacy shocked at the Louvre, but I was strangely tempted to resent as an affront the hint I received, that I might steal a glance at what was deemed indecent. Perhaps the arrangements for the exhibition of this room, the feelings which have led to them, and the result they have produced, furnish as good a specimen of the kind of delicacy on which the Americans pride themselves, and of the peculiarities arising from it, as can be found. The room contains about fifty casts, chiefly from the antique. . . .

II, 86

Market in Philadelphia

II, 98

I was particularly requested to visit the market of Philadelphia, at the hour when it presented the busiest scene; I did so, and thought few cities had any thing to show better worth looking at; it is, indeed, the very perfection of a market, the *beau ideal* of a notable housewife, who would confide to no deputy the important office of caterer. The neatness, freshness, and entire absence of every thing disagreeable to sight or smell, must be witnessed to be believed. The stalls were spread with snow-white napkins; flowers and fruit, if not quite of Paris or London perfection, yet bright, fresh, and fragrant; with excellent vegetables in the greatest variety and abundance, were all so delightfully exhibited, that objects less pleasing were overlooked and forgotten. The dairy, the poultry-yard, the forest, the river, and the ocean, all contributed their spoil; in short, for the first time in my life, I thought a market a beautiful object. The prices of most articles were, as nearly as I could calculate between dollars and francs, about the same as at Paris; certainly much cheaper than in London, but much dearer than at Exeter.

My letters of introduction brought me acquainted with several amiable and interesting people. There is something in the tone of manners at Philadelphia that I liked; it appeared to me that there was less affectation of ton there than elsewhere. There is a quietness, a composure in a / Philadelphia drawing-room, that is quite characteristic of a city founded by William Penn. The dress of the ladies, even those who are not Quakers, partakes of this; they are most elegantly neat, and there was a delicacy and good taste in the dress of the young ladies that might serve as a model to the whole Union. There can hardly be a stronger contrast in the style of dress between any two cities than may be remarked between Baltimore and Philadelphia; both are costly, but the former is distinguished by gaudy splendour, the latter by elegant simplicity.

II, 99

It is said that this city has many gentlemen distinguished by their scientific pursuits; I conversed with several well-informed and intelligent men, but there is a cold dryness of manner and an apparent want of interest in the subjects they discuss, that, to my mind, robs conversation of all its charm. On one occasion I heard the character and situation of an illustrious officer discussed, who had served with renown under Napoleon, and whose high character might have obtained him favour under the Bourbons, could he have abandoned the principles which led him to dislike their / government. (II, 100) This distinguished man had retreated to America after the death of his master, and was endeavoring to establish a sort of Polytechnic academy at New York: in speaking of him, I observed, that his devotion to the cause of freedom must prove a strong recommendation in the United States. "Not the least in the world, madam," answered a gentleman who ranked deservedly high among the *literati* of the city, "it might avail him much in England, perhaps, but here we are perfectly indifferent as to what people's principles may be."

This I believe to be exactly true, though I never before heard it avowed as a national feature.

The want of warmth, of interest, of feeling, upon all subjects which do not immediately touch their own concerns, is universal, and has a most paralysing effect upon conversation. All the enthusiasm of America is concentrated to the one point of her own emancipation and independence; on this point nothing can exceed the warmth of her feelings. She may, I think, be compared to a young bride, a sort of Mrs. Major Waddle; her independence is to her as a newly-won / bridegroom; (II, 101) for him alone she has eyes, ears, or heart; — the honeymoon is not over yet; — when it is, America will, perhaps, learn more coquetry, and know better how to *faire l'aimable* to other nations.

I conceive that no place in the known world can furnish so striking a proof of the immense value of literary habits as the United States, not only in enlarging the mind, but what is of infinitely more importance, in purifying the manners. During my abode in the country I not only never met a literary man who was a tobacco chewer or a whiskey-drinker, but I never met any who were not, that had escaped these degrading habits. On the women, the influence is, if possible, still more important; unfortunately, the instances are rare, but they are to be found. One admirable example occurs in the person of a young lady of Cincinnati; surrounded by a society totally incapable of appreciating, or even of comprehending her, she holds a place among it, as simply and unaffectedly as if of the same species; young, beautiful, and gifted by nature with a mind singularly acute and discriminating, she has happily / found such opportunities (II, 102) of cultivation as might distinguish her in any country; it is, indeed, that best of all cultivation which is only to be found in domestic habits of literature, and in that hourly education which the daughter of a man of letters receives when she is made the companion and friend of her father. This young lady is the more admirable as she contrives to unite all the multifarious duties which usually devolve upon American ladies, with her intellectual pursuits. The companion and efficient assistant of her father's literary labours, the active aid in all the household cares of her mother, the tender nurse of a delicate infant sister, the skilful artificer of her own always elegant wardrobe, ever at leisure, and ever prepared to receive with the sweetest cheerfulness her numerous acquaintance, the most animated in conversation, the most indefatigable in occupation, it was impossible to know her, and study her character, without feeling that such women were "the glory of all lands," and, could the race be multiplied, would speedily become the reformers of all the grossness and ignorance that now degrade her own. Is it to be imagined, that if fifty / modifications of this (II, 103) charming young woman were to be met at a party, the men would dare to enter it reeking with whiskey, their lips blackened with tobacco, and convinced, to the very centre of their hearts and souls, that women were made for no other purpose than to fabricate sweetmeats and gingerbread, construct shirts, darn stockings, and become mothers of possible presidents? Assuredly not. Should the women of America ever discover what their power might be, and compare it with what it is, much improvement might be hoped for. While, at Philadelphia, among the handsomest, the wealthiest, and the most distinguished of the land, their comparative influence in society with that possessed in Europe by females holding the same station, occurred forcibly to my mind. . . .

City of New York

II, 189 New York, indeed, appeared to us, even when we saw it by a soberer light, a lovely and a noble city. To us who had been so long travelling through half-cleared forests, and sojourning among an "I'm-as-good-as-you" population, it seemed, perhaps, more beautiful, more splendid, and more refined than it might have done, had we arrived there directly from London; but making every allowance for this, I must still declare that I think New York one of the finest cities I ever saw, and as much superior to every other in the Union (Philadelphia not excepted), as London to Liverpool, or Paris to Rouen. Its advantages of position are, perhaps, unequalled any where. Situated on an island, which I think it will one day cover, it rises like Venice, from the sea, and like that fairest of cities in the days of her glory, receives into its lap tribute of all the riches of the earth.

The southern point of Manhatten Island divides / the waters of the harbour into the North and East rivers; on this point stands the city of New York extending from river to river, and running northward to the extent of three or four miles. I think it covers nearly as much ground as Paris, but is much less thickly peopled. The extreme point is fortified towards the sea by a battery, and forms an admirable point of defence; but in these piping days of peace, it is converted into a public promenade, and one more beautiful, I should suppose, no city could boast. From hence commences the splendid Broadway, as the fine avenue is called which runs through the whole city. This noble street may vie with any I ever saw, for its length and breadth, its handsome shops, neat awnings, excellent *trottoir,* and well-dressed pedestrians. It has not the crowded glitter of Bond-street equipages, nor the gorgeous fronted palaces of Regent-street; but it is magnificent in its extent, and ornamented by several handsome buildings, some of them surrounded by grass and trees. The Park, in which stands the noble city-hall, is a very fine area. I never found that the most graphic description of a city could give me / any feeling of being there; and even if others have the power, I am very sure I have not, of setting churches and squares, and long drawn streets, before the mind's eye. I will not, therefore, attempt a detailed description of this great metropolis of the new world, but will only say that during the seven weeks we stayed there, we always found something new to see and to admire; and were it not so very far from all the old-world things which cling about the heart of an European, I should say that I never saw a city more desirable as a residence.

(II, 190; II, 191)

The dwelling houses of the higher classes are extremely handsome, and very richly furnished. Silk or satin furniture is as often, or oftener, seen than chintz; the mirrors are as handsome as in London; the cheffoniers, slabs, and marble tables as elegant; and in addition, they have all the pretty tasteful decoration of French porcelaine, and or-molu in much greater abundance, because at a much cheaper rate. Every part of their houses is well carpeted, and the exterior finishing, such as steps, railings, and door-frames, are very superior. Almost every house has handsome / green blinds on the outside; balconies are not very general, nor do the houses display, externally, so many flowers as those of Paris and London; but I saw many rooms decorated within, exactly like those of an European *petite maîtresse.*[1] Little tables, looking and

(II, 192)

[1] Woman of high style or fashion.

smelling like flower beds, portfolios, nicknacks, bronzes, busts, cameos, and alabaster vases, illustrated copies of ladylike rhymes bound in silk, and, in short, all the pretty coxcomalities of the drawing-room scattered about with the same profuse and studied negligence as with us.

Hudson Square and its neighbourhood is, I believe, the most fashionable part of the town; the square is beautiful, excellently well planted with a great variety of trees, and only wanting our frequent and careful mowing to make it equal to any square in London. The iron railing which surrounds this enclosure is as high and as handsome as that of the Tuilleries, and it will give some idea of the care bestowed on its decoration, to know that the gravel for the walks was conveyed by barges from Boston, not as ballast, but as freight.

II, 193 The great defect in the houses is their extreme uniformity—when you have seen one, you have seen all. Neither do I quite like the arrangement of the rooms. In nearly all the houses the dining and drawing-rooms are on the same floor, with ample folding doors between them; when thrown together they certainly make a very noble apartment; but no doors can be barrier sufficient between dining and drawing-rooms. Mixed dinner parties of ladies and gentlemen, however, are very rare, which is a great defect in the society; not only as depriving them of the most social and hospitable manner of meeting, but as leading to frequent dinner parties of gentlemen without ladies, which certainly does not conduce to refinement.

The evening parties, excepting such as are expressly for young people, are chiefly conversational; we were too late in the season for large parties, but we saw enough to convince us that there is society to be met with in New York, which would be deemed delightful any where. Cards are very seldom used; and music, from their having very little professional aid at their / II, 194 parties, is seldom, I believe, as good as what is heard at private concerts in London.

The Americans have certainly not the same *besoin* of being amused, as other people; they may be the wiser for this, perhaps, but it makes them less agreeable to a looker-on.

There are three theatres at New York, all of which we visited. The Park Theatre is the only one licensed by fashion, but the Bowery is infinitely superior in beauty; it is indeed as pretty a theatre as I ever entered, perfect as to size and proportion, elegantly decorated, and the scenery and machinery equal to any in London, but it is not the fashion. The Chatham is so utterly condemned by *bon ton,* that it requires some courage to decide upon going there; nor do I think my curiosity would have penetrated so far, had I not seen Miss Mitford's Rienzi advertised there. It was the first opportunity I had had of seeing it played, and spite of very indifferent acting, I was delighted. The interest must have been great, for till the curtain fell, I saw not one quarter of the queer things around me: then I observed in the front row of a dressbox a lady performing the / most II, 195 maternal office possible; several gentlemen without their coats, and a general air of contempt for the decencies of life, certainly more than usually revolting.

At the Park Theatre I again saw the American Roscius, Mr. Forrest. He played the part of Damon, and roared, I thought, very unlike a nightingale. I cannot admire this celebrated performer.

Another night we saw Cinderella there; Mrs. Austin was the prima donna, and much admired. The piece was extremely well got up, and on this occasion we saw the Park Theatre to advantage, for it was filled with well-dressed company; but still we saw many "yet unrazored lips" polluted with the grim tinge of the hateful tobacco, and heard, without ceasing, the spitting, which of course is its consequence. If their theatres had the orchestra of the Feydeau, and a choir of angels to boot, I could find but little pleasure, so long as they were followed by this running accompaniment of *thorough base.*

Charles Dickens

From *American Notes for General Circulation* by Charles Dickens. Paris (Stassin and Xavier), 1842.

No contemporary traveler received the welcome that Charles Dickens enjoyed on his visit to the United States. Already known and celebrated for such books as *Pickwick Papers, Oliver Twist,* and *Nicholas Nickleby,* the English novelist was feted and flattered throughout his tour. However, the publication of *American Notes* (1842) aroused substantial American resentment despite the fact that Dickens found much that was admirable in American life. The major sources of trouble were his condemnation of slavery, his criticism of the penal system, and his strong complaint over the lack of copyright laws in the country. Actually, if *American Notes* is kept separate from *Martin Chuzzlewit* (1843–1844) Dickens's judgment of America was little if any harsher than that of the average English visitor. He differed from ordinary observers only in the crispness of his comments and in the vivacity of his impressions. True to his literary method he seized on the unusual and the comic rather than the pedestrian. Unfortunately, Americans who enjoyed the caricaturing of Englishmen in Dickens's works did not relish the idea of having Dickens's art in this respect turned back on themselves. By the time he returned to the United States in the late 1860's the reaction against him had long since passed and again he was given a most cordial reception.

Boston

31 In all the public establishments of America the utmost courtesy prevails. Most of our Departments are susceptible of considerable improvement in this respect, but the Custom-house, above all others, would do well to take example from the United States, and render itself somewhat less odious and offensive to foreigners. The servile rapacity of the French officials is sufficiently contemptible, but there is a surly, boorish incivility about our men, alike disgusting to all persons who fall into their hands, and discreditable to the nation that keeps such ill-conditioned curs snarling about its gates.

When I landed in America, I could not help being strongly impressed with the contrast their Custom-house presented, and the attention, politeness, and good humour with which its officers discharged their duty.

As we did not land at Boston, in consequence of some detention at the wharf, until after dark, I received my first impressions of the city in walking down to the Custom-house on the morning after our arrival, which was Sunday. I am afraid to say, by-the-way, how many offers of pews and seats in church for that morning were made to us, by formal note of invitation, before we had half finished our first dinner in America, but, if I may be allowed to make a moderate guess, without going into nicer calculation, I should say that, at least, as many sittings were proffered us as would have accommodated a score or two / of 32 grown-up families. The number of creeds and forms of religion to which the pleasure of our company was requested was in very fair proportion.

Not being able, in the absence of any change of clothes, to go to church that day, we were compelled to decline these kindnesses one and all; and I was reluctantly obliged to forego the delight of hearing Dr. Channing, who happened to preach that morning for the first time in a very long interval. I mention the name of this distinguished and accomplished man (with whom I soon afterward had the pleasure of becoming personally acquainted), that I may have the gratification of recording my humble tribute of admiration and respect for his high abilities and character, and for the bold philanthropy with which he has ever opposed himself to that most hideous blot and foul disgrace – Slavery.

To return to Boston. When I got into the streets upon this Sunday morning, the air was so clear, the houses were so bright and gay, the signboards were painted in such gaudy colours, the gilded letters were so very golden, the bricks were so very red, the stone was so very white, the blinds and area railings were so very green, the knobs and plates upon the street-doors so marvellously bright and twinkling, and all so slight and unsubstantial in appearance, that every thoroughfare in the city looked exactly like a scene in a pantomime. It rarely happens in the business streets that a tradesman, if I may venture to call anybody a tradesman, where everybody is a merchant, resides above his store, so that many occupations are carried on in one house, and the whole front is covered with boards and inscriptions. As I walked along, I kept glancing up at these boards, confidently expecting to see a few of them change into something; and I never turned a corner suddenly without looking out for the clown and pantaloon, who, I had no doubt, were hiding in a doorway or behind some pillar close at hand. As to Harlequin and Columbine, I discovered immediately that they lodged (they are always looking after lodgings in a pantomime) at a very small clock-maker's, one story high, near the hotel; which, in 33 addition to various symbols and / devices, almost covering the whole front, had a great dial hanging out – to be jumped through, of course.

The suburbs are, if possible, even more unsubstantial-looking than the city. The white wooden houses (so white that it makes one wink to look at them), with their green jalousie blinds, are so sprinkled and dropped about in all directions, without seeming to have any root at all in the ground, and the small churches and chapels are so prim, and bright, and highly varnished, that I almost believed the whole affair could be taken up piecemeal like a child's toy, and crammed into a little box.

The city is a beautiful one, and cannot fail, I should imagine, to impress all strangers very favourably. The private dwelling-houses are, for the most part, large and elegant, the shops extremely good, and the public buildings handsome. The State House is built upon the summit of a hill, which rises gradually at first, and afterward by a steep ascent, almost from the water's edge. In front is a green enclosure, called the Common. The site is beautiful, and from the top there is a charming panoramic view of the whole town and neighbourhood. In addition to a variety of commodious offices, it contains two handsome chambers: in one the House of Representatives of the State hold their meetings, in the other, the Senate. Such proceedings as I saw here were conducted with perfect gravity and decorum, and were certainly calculated to inspire attention and respect.

There is no doubt that much of the intellectual refinement and superiority of Boston is referable to the quiet influence of the University of Cambridge, which is within three or four miles of the city. The resident professors at that university are gentlemen of learning and varied attainments, and are, without one exception that I can call to mind, men who would shed a grace upon, and do honour to, any society in the civilized world. Many of the resident gentry in Boston and its neighbourhood, and I think I am not mistaken in adding a large majority of those who are attached to the liberal professions there, have been educated at this same school. Whatever the defects of American universities may be, they disseminate / no prejudices; rear no bigots; dig up 34 the buried ashes of no old superstitions; never interpose between the people and their improvement; exclude no man because of his religious opinions; above all, in their whole course of study and instruction, recognise a world, and a broad one too, lying beyond the college walls.

It was a source of inexpressible pleasure to me to observe the almost imperceptible, but not less certain effect wrought by this institution among the small community of Boston, and to note at every turn the humanizing tastes and desires it has engendered; the affectionate friendships to which it has given rise; the amount of vanity and prejudice it has dispelled. The golden calf they worship at Boston is a pigmy compared with the giant effigies set up in other parts of that vast counting-house which lies beyond the Atlantic; and the almighty dollar sinks into something comparatively insignificant amid a whole Pantheon of better gods.

Above all, I sincerely believe that the public institutions and charities of this capital of Massachusetts are as nearly perfect as the most considerate wisdom, benevolence, and humanity can make them. I never in my life was more affected by the contemplation of happiness, under circumstances of privation and bereavement, than in my visits to these establishments.

It is a great and pleasant feature of all such institutions in America, that they are either supported by the State or assisted by the State, or (in the event of their not needing its helping hand) that they act in concert with it, and are emphatically the people's. I cannot but think, with a view to the principle and its tendency to elevate or depress the character of the industrious classes, that a Public Charity is immeasurably better than a Private Foundation, no matter how munificently the latter may be endowed. In our own country, where it has not, until recently, been a very popular fashion with governments to display any extraordinary regard for the great mass of the people, or to recognize their existence as improvable creatures, private charities, unexampled in the history of the earth, 35 have arisen, to do an incalculable amount / of good among the destitute and afflicted. But the government of the country, having neither act nor part in them, is not in the receipt of any portion of the gratitude they inspire and, offering very little shelter or relief beyond that which is to be found in the workhouse and the jail, has come, not unnaturally, to be looked upon by the poor rather as a stern master, quick to correct and punish, than a kind protector, merciful and vigilant in their hour of need. . . .

66 The tone of society, in Boston, is one of perfect politeness, courtesy, and good breeding. The ladies are unquestionably very beautiful – in face: but there I am compelled to stop. Their education is much as with us; neither better nor worse. I had heard some very marvellous stories in this respect; but not believing them, was not disappointed. Blue ladies there are, in Boston; but like philosophers of that colour and sex in most other latitudes, they rather desire to be thought superior than to be so. Evangelical ladies there are, likewise, whose attachment to the forms of religion, and horror of theatrical entertainments, are most exemplary. Ladies who have a passion / 67 for attending lectures are to be found among all classes and all conditions. In the kind of provincial life which prevails in cities such as this, the Pulpit has great influence. The peculiar province of the Pulpit in New England (always excepting the Unitarian ministry) would appear to be the denouncement of all innocent and rational amusements. The church, the chapel, and the lecture-room, are the only means of excitement excepted; and to the church, the chapel, and the lecture-room, the ladies resort in crowds.

Wherever religion is resorted to, as a strong drink, and as an escape from the dull, monotonous round of home, those of its ministers who pepper the highest will be the surest to please. They who strew the Eternal Path with the greatest amount of brimstone, and who most ruthlessly tread down the flowers and leaves that grow by the way-side, will be voted the most righteous; and they who enlarge with the greatest pertinacity on the difficulty of getting into heaven, will be considered, by all true believers, certain of going there: though it would be hard to say by what process of reasoning this conclusion is arrived at. It is so at home, and it is so abroad. With regard to the other means of excitement, the Lecture, it has at least the merit of being always new. One lecture treads so quickly on the heels of another, that none are remembered; and the course of this month may be safely repeated next, with its charm of novelty unbroken, and its interest unabated. . . .

70 Having passed the time I spent in Boston . . . in . . . mixing constantly with its society, I am not aware that I have any occasion to prolong this chapter. Such of its social customs as I have not mentioned, however, may be told in a very few words.

The usual dinner-hour is two o'clock. A dinner party takes place at five; and at an evening party, they seldom sup later than eleven; so that it goes hard but one gets home, even from a rout, by midnight. I never could find out any difference between a party at Boston and a party in London, saving that at the former place all assemblies are held at more rational hours; that the conversation may possibly be a little louder and more cheerful; that a guest is usually expected to ascend to the very top of the house to take his cloak off; that he is certain to see at every dinner an unusual amount of poultry on the table; and at every supper, at least two mighty bowls of hot stewed oysters, in any one of which a half-grown Duke of Clarence might be smothered easily.

There are two theatres in Boston, of good size and construction, but sadly in want of patronage. The few ladies who resort to them sit, as of right, in the front rows of the boxes. . . .

Lowell

75 Before leaving Boston, I devoted one day to an excursion to Lowell. I assign a separate chapter to this visit; not because I am about to describe it at any length, but because I remember it as a thing by itself, and am desirous that my readers should do the same.

I made acquaintance with an American railroad, on this occasion, for the first time. As these works are pretty much alike all through the States, their general characteristics are easily described.

There are no first and second class carriages as with us; but there is a gentlemen's car and a ladies' car; the main distinction between which is that in the first, everybody smokes; and in the second, nobody does. As a black man never travels with a white one, there is also a negro car; which is a great blundering clumsy chest, such as Gulliver put to sea in, from the kingdom of Brobdignag. There is a great deal of jolting, a great deal of noise, a great deal of wall, not much window, a locomotive engine, a shriek, and a bell.

The cars are like shabby omnibuses, but larger; holding thirty, forty, fifty, people. The seats, instead of stretching from end to end, are placed crosswise. Each seat holds two persons. There is a long row of them on each side of the caravan, a narrow passage up the middle, and a door at both ends. In the centre of the carriage there is usually a stove, fed / with charcoal or anthracite 76 coal; which is for the most part red-hot. It is insufferably close; and you see the hot air fluttering between yourself and any other object you may happen to look at, like the ghost of smoke.

In the ladies' car, there are a great many gentlemen who have ladies with them. There are also a great many ladies who have nobody with them; for any lady may travel alone, from one end of the United States to the other, and be certain of the most courteous and considerate treatment everywhere. The conductor or check-taker, or guard, or whatever he may be, wears no uniform. He walks up and down the car, and in and out of it, as his fancy dictates; leans against the door with his hands in his pockets and stares at you, if you chance to be a stranger; or enters into conversation with the passengers about him. A great many newspapers are pulled out, and a few of them are read. Everybody talks to you, or to anybody else who hits his fancy. If you are an Englishman, he expects that that railroad is pretty much like an English railroad. If you say "No," he says "Yes?" (interrogatively,) and asks in what respect they differ. You enumerate the heads of difference, one by one, and he says "Yes?" (still interrogatively) to each. Then he guesses that you don't travel faster in England; and on your replying that you do, says "Yes?" again (still interrogatively), and, it is quite evident, don't believe it. After a long pause he remarks, partly to you, and partly to the knob on the top of his stick, that "Yankees are reckoned to be considerable of a go-ahead people too;" upon which *you* say "Yes," and then *he* says "Yes" again (affirmatively this time); and upon your looking out of window, tells you that behind that hill, and some three miles from the next station, there is a clever town in a smart lo-ca-tion, where he expects you have concluded to stop. Your answer in the negative naturally leads to more questions in reference to your intended route (always pronounced rout); and wherever you are going, you invariably learn that you can't get there without immense difficulty and danger, and that all the great sights are somewhere else.

If a lady take a fancy to any male passenger's seat, the gentleman / 77 who accompanies her gives him notice of the fact, and he immediately vacates it with great politeness. Politics are much discussed, so are banks, so is cotton. Quiet people avoid the question of the Presidency, for there will be a new election in three years and a half, and party feeling runs very high: the great constitutional feature of this institution being, that directly the acrimony of the last election is over, the acrimony of the next one begins; which is an unspeakable comfort to all strong politicians and true lovers of their country: that is to say, to ninety-nine men and boys out of every ninety-nine and a quarter.

Except when a branch road joins the main one, there is seldom more than one track of rails; so that the road is very narrow, and the view, where there is a deep cutting, by no means extensive. When there is not, the character of the scenery is always the same. Mile after mile of stunted trees: some hewn down by the axe, some blown down by the wind, some half fallen and resting on their neighbours, many mere logs half hidden in the swamp, others mouldered away to spongy chips. The very soil of the earth is made up of minute fragments such as these; each pool of stagnant water has its crust of vegetable rottenness; on every side there are the boughs, and trunks, and stumps of trees, in every possible stage of decay, decomposition, and neglect. Now you emerge for a few brief minutes on an open country, glittering with some bright lake or pool, broad as many an English river, but so small here that it scarcely has a name; now catch hasty glimpses of a distant town, with its clean white houses and their cool piazzas, its prim New-England church and schoolhouse; when whir-r-r-r! almost before you have seen them, comes the same dark screen: the stunted trees, the stumps, the logs, the stagnant water – all so like the last that you seem to have been transported back again by magic.

The train calls at stations in the woods, where the wild impossibility of anybody having the smallest reason to get out, is only to be equalled by the apparently desperate hopelessness of there being anybody to get in. It rushes across the turnpike / 78 road, where there is no gate, no policeman, no signal: nothing but a rough wooden arch, on which is painted *"When the bell rings, look out for the Locomotive."* On it whirls headlong, dives through the woods again, emerges in the light, clatters over frail arches, rumbles upon the heavy ground, shoots beneath a wooden bridge which intercepts the light for a second like a wink, suddenly awakens all the slumbering echoes in the main street of a large town, and dashes on hap-hazard, pell-mell, neck or nothing, down the middle of the road. There – with mechanics working at their trades, and people leaning from their doors and windows, and boys flying kites and playing marbles, and men smoking, and women talking, and children crawling, and pigs burrowing, and unaccustomed horses plunging and rearing, close to the very rails – there – on, on, on – tears the mad dragon of an engine with its train of cars; scattering in all directions a shower of burning sparks from its wood fire; screeching, hissing, yelling, panting: until at last the thirsty monster stops beneath a covered way to drink, the people cluster round, and you have time to breathe again.

I was met at the station at Lowell by a gentleman intimately connected with the management of the factories there; and gladly putting myself under his guidance, drove off at once to that quarter of the town in which the works, the object of my visit, were situated. Although only just of age – for if my recollection serve me, it has been a manufacturing town barely one-and-twenty years – Lowell is a large, populous, thriving place. Those indications of its youth which first attract the eye, give it a quaintness and oddity of character which, to a visitor from the old country, is amusing enough. It was a very dirty winter's day, and nothing in the whole town looked old to me, except the mud, which in some parts was almost knee-deep, and might have been deposited there on the subsiding of the waters after the Deluge. In one place, there was a new wooden church, which, having no steeple, and being yet unpainted, looked like an enormous packing-case without any direction upon it. In another there was a large hotel, whose walls and colonnades were so crisp, and thin, and slight, that / it had exactly the appearance of being built with cards. I was careful not to draw my breath as we passed, and trembled when I saw a workman come out upon the roof, lest with one thoughtless stamp of his foot he should crush the structure beneath him, and bring it rattling down. The very river that moves the machinery in the mills (for they are all worked by water power), seems to acquire a new character from the fresh buildings of bright red brick and painted wood among which it takes its course; and to be as light-headed, thoughtless, and brisk a young river, in its murmurings and tumblings, as one would desire to see. One would swear that every "Bakery," "Grocery," and "Bookbindery," and other kind of store, took its shutters down for the first time, and started in business yesterday. The golden pestles and mortars fixed as signs upon the sun blind frames outside the druggist's, appear to have been just turned out of the United States' Mint; and when I saw a baby of some week or ten days old in a woman's arms at a street corner, I found myself unconsciously wondering where it came from: never supposing for an instant that it could have been born in such a young town as that.

There are several factories in Lowell, each of which belongs to what we should term a Company of Proprietors, but what they call in America a Corporation. I went over several of these; such as a woolen factory, a carpet factory, and a cotton factory: examined them in every part; and saw them in their ordinary working aspect, with no preparation of any kind, or departure from their ordinary every-day proceedings. I may add that I am well acquainted with our manufacturing towns in England, and have visited many mills in Manchester and elsewhere in the same manner.

I happened to arrive at the first factory just as the dinner-hour was over, and the girls were returning to their work; indeed, the stairs of the mill were thronged with them as I ascended. They were all well-dressed, but not to my thinking above their condition: for I like to see the humbler classes of society careful of their dress and appearance, and even, if they please, decorated with such little trinkets as come within the / compass of their means. Supposing it confined within reasonable limits, I would always encourage this kind of pride, as a worthy element of self-respect, in any person I employed; and should no more be deterred from doing so, because some wretched female referred her fall to a love

79

80

of dress, than I would allow my construction of the real intent and meaning of the Sabbath to be influenced by any warning to the well-disposed, founded on his backslidings on that particular day, which might emanate from the rather doubtful authority of a murderer in Newgate.

These girls, as I have said, were all well dressed: and that phrase necessarily includes extreme cleanliness. They had serviceable bonnets, good warm cloaks, and shawls; and were not above clogs and pattens. Moreover, there were places in the mill in which they could deposite these things without injury; and there were conveniences for washing. They were healthy in appearance, many of them remarkably so, and had the manners and deportment of young women: not of degraded brutes of burden. If I had seen in one of those mills (but I did not, though I looked for something of this kind with a sharp eye), the most lisping, mincing, affected, and ridiculous young creature that my imagination could suggest, I should have thought of the careless, moping, slatternly, degraded, dull reverse (I *have* seen that), and should have been still well pleased to look upon her.

The rooms in which they worked were as well ordered as themselves. In the windows of some there were green plants, which were trained to shade the glass; in all, there was as much fresh air, cleanliness, and comfort as the nature of the occupation would possibly admit of. Out of so large a number of females, many of whom were only then just verging upon womanhood, it may be reasonably supposed that some were delicate and fragile in appearance: no doubt there were. But I solemnly declare, that from all the crowd I saw in the different factories that day, I cannot recall or separate one young face that gave me a painful impression; not one young girl whom, assuming it to be matter of necessity that she should / 81 gain her daily bread by the labour of her hands, I would have removed from those works if I had had the power.

They reside at various boarding-houses near at hand. The owners of the mills are particularly careful to allow no persons to enter upon the possession of these houses, whose characters have not undergone the most searching and thorough inquiry. Any complaint that is made against them by the boarders or by anybody else, is fully investigated; and if good ground of complaint be shown to exist against them, they are removed, and their occupation is handed over to some more deserving person. There are a few children employed in these factories, but not many. The laws of the State forbid their working more than nine months in the year, and require that they be educated during the other three. For this purpose there are schools in Lowell; and there are churches and chapels of various persuasions, in which the young women may observe that form of Worship in which they have been educated.

At some distance from the factories, and on the highest and pleasantest ground in the neighbourhood, stands their hospital, or boarding-house for the sick: it is the best house in those parts, and was built by an eminent merchant for his own residence. Like that institution at Boston which I have before described, it is not parcelled out into wards, but is divided into convenient chambers, each of which has all the comforts of a very comfortable home. The principal medical attendant resides under the same roof; and were the patients members of his own family, they could not be better cared for, or attended with greater gentleness and consideration. The weekly charge in this establishment for each patient is three dollars, or twelve shillings English; but no girl employed by any of the corporations is ever excluded for want of the means of payment. That they do not very often want the means, may be gathered from the fact, that in July, 1841, no fewer than nine hundred and seventy-eight of these girls were depositors in the Lowell Savings Bank: the amount of whose joint savings was estimated at one hundred thousand dollars, or twenty thousand English pounds.

I am now going to state three facts, which 82

will startle a large class of readers on this side of the Atlantic, very much.

Firstly, there is a joint-stock piano in a great many of the boarding-houses. Secondly, nearly all these young ladies subscribe to circulating libraries. Thirdly, they have got up among themselves a periodical called *The Lowell Offering*, "A repository of original articles, written exclusively by females actively employed in the mills," which is duly printed, published, and sold; and whereof I brought away from Lowell four hundred good solid pages, which I have read from beginning to end.

The large class of readers, startled by these facts will exclaim, with one voice, "How very preposterous!" On my deferentially inquiring why, they will answer, "These things are above their station." In reply to that objection, I would beg to ask what their station is.

It is their station to work. And they *do* work. They labour in these mills, upon an average, twelve hours a day, which is unquestionably work, and pretty tight work too. Perhaps it is above their station to indulge in such amusements, on any terms. Are we quite sure that we in England have not formed our ideas of the "station" of working people, from accustoming ourselves to the contemplation of that class as they are, and not as they might be? I think that if we examine our own feelings, we shall find that the pianos, and the circulating-libraries, and even *The Lowell Offering*, startle us by their novelty, and not by their bearing upon any abstract question of right or wrong.

For myself, I know no station in which, the occupation of to-day cheerfully done and the occupation of to-morrow cheerfully looked to, any one of these pursuits is not most humanizing and laudable. I know no station which is rendered more endurable to the person in it, or more safe to the person out of it, by having ignorance for its associate. I know no station which has a right to monopolize the means of mutual instruction, improvement, and rational entertainment; or which has ever continued to be a station very long, after seeking to do so.

83 Of the merits of *The Lowell Offering* as a literary production, I will only observe, putting entirely out of sight the fact of the articles having been written by these girls after the arduous labours of the day, that it will compare advantageously with a great many English Annuals. It is pleasant to find that many of its Tales are of the Mills and of those who work in them; that they inculcate habits of self-denial and contentment, and teach good doctrines of enlarged benevolence. A strong feeling for the beauties of nature, as displayed in the solitudes the writers have left at home, breathes through its pages like wholesome village air; and though a circulating library is a favourable school for the study of such topics, it has very scanty allusion to fine clothes, fine marriages, fine houses, or fine life. Some persons might object to the papers being signed occasionally with rather fine names, but this is an American fashion. One of the provinces of the state legislature of Massachusetts is to alter ugly names into pretty ones, as the children improve upon the tastes of their parents. These changes costing little or nothing, scores of Mary Annes are solemnly converted into Bevelinas every session.

It is said that on the occasion of a visit from General Jackson or General Harrison to this town (I forget which, but it is not to the purpose), he walked through three miles and a half of these young ladies, all dressed out with parasols and silk stockings. But as I am not aware that any worse consequence ensued, than a sudden looking-up of all the parasols and silk stockings in the market; and perhaps the bankruptcy of some speculative New-Englander who bought them all up at one price, in expectation of a demand that never came; I set no great store by the circumstance.

In this brief account of Lowell, and inadequate expression of the gratification it yielded me, and cannot fail to afford to any foreigner to whom the condition of such people at home is a subject of interest and anxious speculation, I have carefully abstained from drawing a comparison between these factories and those of our own land. Many of the circumstances whose strong influence has been at work for years in our 84 manufacturing / towns have not arisen here; and there is no manufacturing population in Lowell, so to speak: for these girls (often the daughters of small farmers) come from other states, remain a few years in the mills, and then go home for good.

The contrast would be a strong one, for it would be between the Good and Evil, the living light and deepest shadow. I abstain from it, because I deem it just to do so. But I only the more earnestly adjure all those whose eyes may rest on these pages, to pause and reflect upon the difference between this town and those great haunts of desperate misery: to call to mind, if they can in the midst of party strife and squabble, the efforts that must be made to purge them of their suffering and danger: and last, and foremost, to remember how the precious Time is rushing by.

I returned at night by the same railroad and in the same kind of car. One of the passengers being exceedingly anxious to expound at great length to my companion (not to me, of course) the true principles on which books of travel in America should be written by Englishmen, I feigned to fall asleep. But glancing all the way out at window from the corners of my eyes, I found abundance of entertainment for the rest of the ride in watching the effects of the wood fire, which had been invisible in the morning, but were now brought out in full relief by the darkness: for we were travelling in a whirlwind of bright sparks, which showered about us like a storm of fiery snow. . . .

New York

99 The beautiful metropolis of America is by no means so clean a city as Boston, but many of its streets have the same characteristics; except that the houses are not quite so fresh-coloured, the sign-boards are not quite so gaudy, the gilded letters not quite so golden, the bricks not quite so red, the stone not quite so white, the blinds and area railings not quite so green, the knobs and plates upon the street doors, not quite so bright and twinkling. There are many by-streets, almost as neutral in clean colours, and positive in dirty ones, as by-streets in London; and there is one quarter, commonly called the Five Points, which, in respect of filth and wretchedness, may be safely backed against Seven Dials, or any other part of famed St. Giles's.

The great promenade and thoroughfare, as most people know, is Broadway; a wide and bustling street, which, from the Battery Gardens to its opposite termination in a country road, may be four miles long. Shall we sit down in an upper floor of the Carlton House Hotel (situated in the best part of this main artery of New York), and when we are tired of looking down upon the life below, sally forth arm-in-arm, and mingle with the stream?

Warm weather! The sun strikes upon our heads at this open window, as though its rays were concentrated through a / burn- 100 ing-glass; but the day is in its zenith, and the season an unusual one. Was there ever such a sunny street as this Broadway? The pavement stones are polished with the tread of feet until they shine again; the red bricks of the houses might be yet in the dry, hot kilns; and the roofs of those omnibuses look as though, if water were poured on them, they would hiss and smoke, and smell like half-quenched fires. No stint of omnibuses here! Half a dozen have gone by within as many minutes. Plenty of hackney cabs and coaches too; gigs, phaetons, large-wheeled tilburies, and private carriages — rather of a clumsy make, and not very different from the public vehicles, but built for the heavy roads beyond the city pavement. Negro coachmen and white; in straw hats, black hats, white hats, glazed caps, fur caps; in coats of drab, black, brown, green, blue, nankeen, striped jean and linen; and there, in that one instance (look while it passes, or it will be too late), in suits of livery. Some southern republican that, who puts his blacks in uniform, and swells with Sultan pomp and power. Yonder, where that phaeton with the well-clipped pair of grays has stopped – standing at their heads now – is a Yorkshire groom, who has not been very long in these parts, and looks sorrowfully round for a companion pair of top-boots, which he may traverse the city half a year without meeting. Heaven save the ladies, how they dress! We have seen more colours in these ten minutes, than we should have seen elsewhere, in as many days. What various parasols! what rainbow silks and satins! what pinking of thin stockings, and pinching of thin shoes, and fluttering of ribands and silk tassels, and display of rich cloaks with gaudy hoods and linings! The young gentlemen are fond, you see, of turning down their shirt-collars and cultivating their whiskers, especially under the chin; but they cannot approach the ladies in their dress or bearing, being, to say the truth, humanity of quite another sort. Byrons of the desk and counter, pass on, and let us see what kind of men those are behind ye: those two labourers in holyday clothes, of whom one carries in his hand a crumpled scrap of paper from which he tries to spell out a hard name, while the other looks about for it, on all the doors and windows.

101 Irishmen both! You might know them, if they were masked, by their long-tailed blue coats and bright buttons, and their drab trousers, which they wear like men well used to working dresses, who are easy in no others. It would be hard to keep your model republics going, without the countrymen and countrywomen of those two labourers. For who else would dig, and delve, and drudge, and do domestic work, and make canals and roads, and execute great lines of Internal Improvement! Irishmen both, and sorely puzzled too, to find out what they seek. Let us go down, and help them, for the love of home, and that spirit of liberty which admits of honest service to honest men, and honest work for honest bread, no matter what it be.

That's well! We have got at the right address at last, though it is written in strange characters truly, and might have been scrawled with the blunt handle of the spade the writer better knows the use of, than a pen. Their way lies yonder, but what business takes them there? They carry savings: to hoard up? No. They are brothers, those men. One crossed the sea alone, and working very hard for one half year, and living harder, saved funds enough to bring the other out. That done, they worked together, side by side, contentedly sharing hard labour and hard living for another term, and then their sisters came, and then another brother, and, lastly, their old mother. And what now? Why, the poor old crone is restless in a strange land, and yearns to lay her bones, she says, among her people in the old graveyard at home; and so they go to pay her passage back: and God help her and them, and every simple heart, and all who turn to the Jerusalem of their younger days, and have an altar-fire upon the cold hearth of their fathers.

This narrow thoroughfare, baking and blistering in the sun, is Wall Street: the Stock Exchange and Lombard Street of New York. Many a rapid fortune has been made in this street, and many a no less rapid ruin. Some of these very merchants whom you see hanging about here now, have locked up Money in their strongboxes, like the man in the Arabian Nights, and opening them again, have found but withered leaves. / Below, here by the 102 water side, where the bowsprits of ships stretch across the footway, and almost thrust themselves into the windows, lie the noble American vessels which have made their Packet Service the finest in the world. They have brought hither the foreigners who abound in all the streets: not perhaps, that there are more here than in other commercial cities; but elsewhere, they have particular haunts, and you must find them out; here, they pervade the town.

We must cross Broadway again; gaining some refreshment from the heat, in the sight of the great blocks of clean ice which are being carried into shops and bar-rooms; and the pine-apples and water-melons profusely displayed for sale. Fine streets of spacious houses here, you see! – Wall Street has furnished and dismantled many of them very often – and here a deep green leafy square. Be sure that is a hospitable house with inmates to be affectionately remembered always, where they have the open door and pretty show of plants within, and where the child with laughing eyes is peeping out of window at the little dog below. You wonder what may be the use of this tall flagstaff in the by street, with something like Liberty's head-dress on its top: so do I. But there is a passion for tall flagstaffs hereabout, and you may see its twin brother in five minutes, if you have a mind.

Again cross Broadway, and so – passing from the many-coloured crowd and glittering shops – into another long main street, the Bowery. A railroad yonder, see, where two stout horses trot along, drawing a score or two of people and a great wooden ark, with ease. The stores are poorer here; the passengers less gay. Clothes ready-made, and meat ready-cooked, are to be bought in these parts; and the lively whirl of carriages is exchanged for the deep rumble of carts and wagons. The signs which are so plentiful, in shape like river buoys, or small balloons, hoisted by cords to poles, and dangling there, announce, as you may see by looking up, *"Oysters in every Style."* They tempt the hungry most at night, for then dull candles glimmering inside, illuminate these dainty words, and make the mouths of idlers water, as they read and linger. . . .

106 Once more in Broadway! Here are the same ladies in bright colours, walking to and fro in pairs and singly; yonder the very same light blue parasol which passed and repassed the hotel window twenty times while we were sitting there. We are going to cross here. Take care of the pigs. Two portly sows are trotting up behind this carriage, and a select party of half-a-dozen gentlemen-hogs have just now turned the corner.

Here is a solitary swine, lounging homeward by himself. He has only one ear; having parted with the other to vagrant-dogs in the course of his city rambles. But he gets on very well without it; and leads a roving, gentlemanly vagabond kind of life, somewhat answering to that of our club-men at home. He leaves his lodgings every morning at a certain hour, throws himself upon the town, gets through his day in some manner quite satisfactory to himself, and regularly appears at the door of his own house again at night, like the mysterious master of Gil Blas. He is a free-and-easy, careless, indifferent kind of pig, having a very large acquaintance among other pigs of the same character, whom he rather knows by sight than conversation, as he seldom troubles himself to stop and exchange civilities, but goes grunting down the kennel, turning up the news and small-talk of the city, in the shape of cabbage-stalks and offal, and bearing no tails but his own: which is a very short one, for his old enemies, the dogs, have been at that too, and have left him hardly enough to swear by. He is in every respect a republican pig, going wherever he pleases, and mingling with the best society, on an equal, if not superior footing, for every one makes way when he appears, and the haughtiest give him the wall if he prefer it. He is a great philosopher, and seldom moved, unless by the dogs before mentioned. Sometimes, indeed, you may see his small eye twinkling on a slaughtered friend, whose carcase garnishes a butcher's door-post, but he grunts out, "Such is life: all flesh is pork!" buries his nose in the mire again, and waddles down the gutter: comforting himself / 107 with the reflection that there is one snout the less to anticipate stray cabbage-stalks, at any rate.

They are the city scavengers, these pigs.

Ugly brutes they are; having, for the most part, scanty, brown backs, like the lids of old horse-hair trunks: spotted with unwholesome black blotches. They have long, gaunt legs, too, and such peaked snouts, that if one of them could be persuaded to sit for his profile, nobody would recognise it for a pig's likeness. They are never attended upon, or led, or driven, or caught, but are thrown upon their own resources in early life, and become preternaturally knowing in consequence. Every pig knows where he lives, much better than anybody could tell him. At this hour, just as evening is closing in, you will see them roaming towards bed by scores, eating their way to the last. Occasionally, some youth among them who has over-eaten himself, or has been much worried by dogs, trots shrinkingly homeward, like a prodigal son: but this is a rare case: perfect self-possession and self-reliance, and immovable composure, being their foremost attributes.

The streets and shops are lighted now; and as the eye travels down the long thoroughfare, dotted with bright jets of gas, it is reminded of Oxford Street or Piccadilly. Here and there, a flight of broad stone cellar-steps appears, and a painted lamp directs you to the Bowling Saloon, or Ten-Pin alley: Ten-Pins being a game of mingled chance and skill, invented when the legislature passed an act forbidding Nine-Pins. At other downward flights of steps, are other lamps, marking the whereabout of oyster-cellars – pleasant retreats, say I: not only by reason of their wonderful cookery of oysters, pretty nigh as large as cheese-plates (or for thy dear sake, heartiest of Greek Professors!) but because of all kinds of eaters of fish, or flesh, or fowl, in these latitudes, the swallower of oysters alone are not gregarious; but subduing themselves, as it were, to the nature of what they work in, and copying the coyness of the thing they eat, do sit apart in curtained boxes, and consort by twos, not by two hundreds.

But how quiet the streets are! Are there no itinerant / bands; no wind or stringed instruments? No, not one. By day, are there no Punches, Fantoccinis, Dancing-dogs, Jugglers, Conjurors, Orchestrinas, or even Barrel-organs? No, not one. Yes, I remember one. One barrel-organ and a dancing monkey – sportive by nature, but fast fading into a dull, lumpish monkey, of the Utilitarian school. Beyond that, nothing lively; no, not so much as a white mouse in a twirling cage. 108

Are there no amusements? Yes. There is a lecture-room across the way, from which that glare of light proceeds, and there may be evening service for the ladies thrice a week, or oftener. For the young gentlemen, there is the counting-house, the store, the bar-room: the latter, as you may see through these windows, pretty full. Hark! to the clicking sound of hammers breaking lumps of ice, and to the cool gurgling of the pounded bits, as, in the process of mixing, they are poured from glass to glass! No amusements? What are these suckers of cigars and swallowers of strong drinks, whose hats and legs we see in every possible variety of twist, doing, but amusing themselves? What are the fifty newspapers, which those precocious urchins are bawling down the street, and which are kept filed within, what are they but amusements? Not vapid waterish amusements, but good strong stuff; dealing in round abuse and blackguard names; pulling off the roofs of private houses, as the Halting Devil did in Spain; pimping and pandering for all degrees of vicious taste, and gorging with coined lies the most voracious maw; imputing to every man in public life the coarsest and the vilest motives; scaring away from the stabbed and prostrate body-politic, every Samaritan of clear conscience and good deeds; and setting on, with yell and whistle and the clapping of foul hands, the vilest vermin and worst birds of prey. – No amusements! . . .

Washington

141 We left Philadelphia by steamboat at six o'clock one very cold morning, and turned our faces towards Washington.

In the course of this day's journey, as on subsequent occasions, we encountered some Englishmen (small farmers, perhaps, or country publicans at home) who were settled in America, and were travelling on their own affairs. Of all grades and kinds of men that jostle one in the public conveyances of the States, these are often the most intolerable and the most insufferable companions. United to every disagreeable characteristic that the worst kind of American travellers possess, these countrymen of ours display an amount of insolent conceit and cool assumption of superiority quite monstrous to behold. In the coarse familiarity of their approach, and the effrontery of their inquisitiveness (which they are in great haste to assert, as if they panted to revenge themselves upon the decent old restraints of home), they surpass any native specimens that came within my range of observation; and I often grew so patriotic when I saw and heard them, that I would cheerfully have submitted to a reasonable fine, if I could have given any other country in the whole world the honour of claiming them for its children.

As Washington may be called the headquarters of tobacco-tinctured saliva, the time is come when I must confess, without any disguise, that the prevalence of those two odious practices of chewing and expectorating began about this time to be anything but agreeable, and soon became most 142 offensive and / sickening. In all the public places of America this filthy custom is recognised. In the courts of law, the judge has his spittoon, the crier his, the witness his, and the prisoner his: while the jurymen and spectators are provided for, as so many men who, in the course of nature, must desire to spit incessantly. In the hospitals, the students of medicine are requested, by notices upon the wall, to eject their tobacco juice into the boxes provided for that purpose, and not to discolour the stairs. In public buildings visiters are implored, through the same agency, to squirt the essence of their quids, or "plugs," as I have heard them called by gentlemen learned in this kind of sweetmeat, into the national spittoons, and not about the bases of the marble colums. But in some parts this custom is inseparably mixed up with every meal and morning call, and with all the transactions of social life. The stranger, who follows in the track I took myself, will find it in its full bloom and glory, luxuriant in all its alarming recklessness, at Washington. And let him not persuade himself (as I once did, to my shame) that previous tourists have exaggerated its extent. The thing itself is an exaggeration of nastiness, which cannot be outdone.

On board this steamboat, there were two young gentlemen, with shirt-collars reversed as usual, and armed with very big walking sticks; who planted two seats in the middle of the deck, at a distance of some four paces apart; took out their tobacco-boxes, and sat down opposite each other, to chew. In less than a quarter of an hour's time, these hopeful youths had shed about them on the clean boards, a copious shower of yellow rain: clearing, by that means, a kind of magic circle, within whose limits no intruders dared to come, and which they never failed to refresh and refresh before a spot was dry. This being before breakfast, rather disposed me, I confess, to nausea; but looking attentively at one of the expectoraters, I plainly saw that he was young in chewing, and felt inwardly uneasy, himself. A glow of delight came over me at this discovery; and as I marked his face turn paler and paler, and saw the ball of tobacco in his left cheek, quiver with his suppressed agony, while yet he spat, and chewed, and spat again, in emulation of his older friend, I could have fallen on his neck and implored him to go on for hours. . . .

154 The President's mansion is more like an English club-house, both within and without, than any other kind of establishment with which I can compare it. The ornamental ground about it has been laid out in garden walks; they are pretty, and agreeable to the eye; though they have that uncomfortable air of having been made yesterday, which is far from favourable to the display of such beauties.

My first visit to this house was on the morning after my arrival, when I was carried thither by an official gentleman, who was so kind as to charge himself with my presentation to the President.

We entered a large hall, and having twice or thrice rung a bell which nobody answered, walked without farther ceremony through the rooms or the ground floor, as divers other gentlemen (mostly with their hats on, and their hands in their pockets) were doing very leisurely. Some of these had ladies with them, to whom they were showing the premises; others were lounging on the chairs and sofas; others, in a perfect state of exhaustion from listlessness, were yawning drearily. The greater portion of this assemblage were rather asserting their supremacy than doing anything else, as they had no particular business there, that anybody knew of. A few were closely eying the movables, as if to make sure that the President (who was far from popular) had not made away with any of the furniture, or sold the fixtures for his private benefit.

After glancing at these loungers; who were scattered over a pretty drawing-room, opening upon a terrace which commanded a beautiful prospect of the river and the adjacent country; and who were sauntering, too, about a larger state room called the Eastern Drawing-room; we went up stairs into another chamber, where were certain visiters, waiting for audiences. At sight of my conductor, a black in plain clothes and yellow slippers who was gliding noiselessly about, and whispering messages in the ears of the more impatient, made a sign of recognition, and glided off to announce him.

We had previously looked into another chamber fitted all round with a great bare wooden desk or counter, whereon lay files of newspapers, to which sundry gentlemen were referring. But there were no such means of beguiling the time in this / apartment, which was as unpromising and tiresome as any waiting room in one of our public establishments, or any physician's dining-room during his hours of consultation at home. 155

There were some fifteen or twenty persons in the room. One, a tall, wiry, muscular old man, from the west; sunburnt and swarthy; with a brown-white hat on his knees, and a giant umbrella resting between his legs; who sat bolt upright in his chair, frowning steadily at the carpet, and twitching the hard lines about his mouth, as if he had made up his mind to "fix" the President on what he had to say, and wouldn't bate him a grain. Another, a Kentucky farmer, six feet six in height, with his hat on, and his hands under his coat-tails, who leaned against the wall and kicked the floor with his heel, as though he had Time's head under his shoe, and were literally "killing" him. A third, an oval-faced, bilious-looking man, with sleek black hair cropped close, and whiskers and beard shaved down to blue dots, who sucked the head of a thick stick, and from time to time took it out of his mouth, to see how it was getting on. A fourth did nothing but whistle. A fifth did nothing but spit. And indeed all these gentlemen were so very persevering and energetic in this latter particular, and bestowed their favours so abundantly upon the carpet, that I take it for granted the Presidential housemaids have high wages, or, to speak more genteelly, an ample amount of "compensation:" which is the American word for salary, in the case of all public servants.

We had not waited in this room many minutes, before the black messenger returned, and conducted us into another of smaller dimensions, where, at a business-like table covered with papers, sat the President himself. He looked somewhat worn and anxious, and well he might: being at war with everybody – but the expression of his face was mild and pleasant, and his manner was remarkably unaffected, gentlemanly, and agreeable. I thought that in his whole carriage and demeanour, he became his station singularly well.

Being advised that the sensible etiquette 156 of the republican / court, admitted of a traveller, like myself, declining, without any impropriety, an invitation to dinner, which did not reach me until I had concluded my arrangements for leaving Washington some days before that to which it referred, I only returned to this house once. It was on the occasion of one of those general assemblies which are held on certain nights between the hours of nine and twelve o'clock, and are called, rather oddly, Levees.

I went, with my wife, at about ten. There was a pretty dense crowd of carriages and people in the court-yard, and so far as I could make out, there were no very clear regulations for the taking up or setting down of company. There were certainly no policemen to soothe startled horses, either by sawing at their bridles or flourishing truncheons in their eyes; and I am ready to make oath that no inoffensive persons were knocked violently on the head, or poked acutely in their backs or stomachs; or brought to a stand-still by any such gentle means, and then taken into custody for not moving on. But there was no confusion or disorder. Our carriage reached the porch in its turn, without any blustering, swearing, shouting, backing, or other disturbance; and we dismounted with as much ease and comfort as though we had been escorted by the whole Metropolitan Force from A to Z inclusive.

The suite of rooms on the ground-floor were lighted up; and a military band was playing in the hall. In the smaller drawing-room, the centre of a circle of company, were the President and his daughter-in-law, who acted as the lady of the mansion: and a very interesting, graceful and accomplished lady too. One gentleman who stood among this group, appeared to take upon himself the functions of a master of the ceremonies. I saw no other officers or attendants, and none were needed.

The great drawing-room, which I have already mentioned, and the other chambers on the ground-floor, were crowded to excess. The company was not, in our sense of the term, select, for it comprehended persons of very many grades and classes; nor was there any great display of costly attire: indeed some of the costumes may have been, for aught I know, grotesque / enough. But 157 the decorum and propriety of behaviour which prevailed, were unbroken by any rude or disagreeable incident; and every man, even among the miscellaneous crowd in the hall who were admitted without any orders or tickets to look on, appeared to feel that he was a part of the Institution, and was responsible for its preserving a becoming character, and appeared to the best advantage.

That these visiters, too, whatever their station, were not without some refinement of taste and appreciation of intellectual gifts, and gratitude to those men who, by the peaceful exercise of great abilities, shed new charms and associations upon the homes of their countrymen, and elevate their character in other lands, was most earnestly testified by their reception of Washington Irving, my dear friend, who had recently been appointed Minister at the court of Spain, and who was among them that night, in his new character, for the first and last time before going abroad. I sincerely believe that in all the madness of American politics, few public men would have been so earnestly, devotedly, and affectionately caressed, as this most charming writer; and I have seldom respected a public assembly more, than I did this eager throng, when I saw them turning with one mind from noisy orators and officers of state, and flocking with a generous and honest impulse round the man of quiet pursuits; proud in his promotion as reflecting back upon their country; and grateful to him with their whole hearts for the store of graceful fancies he had poured out among them. Long may he dispense such treasures with unsparing hand; and long may they remember him as worthily! . . .

A Night Steamer on the Potomac River

161 We were to proceed in the first instance by steamboat: and as it is usual to sleep on board, in consequence of the starting hour being four o'clock in the morning, we went down to where she lay, at that very uncomfortable time for such expeditions when slippers are most valuable, and a familiar bed, in the perspective of an hour or two, looks uncommonly pleasant.

It is ten o'clock at night: say half past ten, moonlight, warm, and dull enough. The steamer (not unlike a child's Noah's ark in form, with the machinery on the top of the roof) is riding lazily up and down, and bumping clumsily against the wooden pier, as the ripple of the river trifles with its unwieldy carcase. The wharf is some distance from the city. There is nobody down here; and one or two dull lamps upon the steamer's decks are the only signs of life remaining, when our coach has driven away. As soon as our footsteps are heard upon the planks, a fat negress, particularly favoured by Nature in respect of bustle, emerges from some dark stairs, and marshals my wife towards the ladies' cabin, to which retreat she goes, followed by a mighty bale of cloaks and great coats. I valiantly resolve not to go to bed at all, but to walk up and down the pier till morning.

I begin my promenade – thinking of all 162 kinds of distant things / and persons, and of nothing near – and pace up and down for half an hour. Then I go on board again; and getting into the light of one of the lamps, look at my watch, and think it must have stopped; and wonder what has become of the faithful secretary whom I brought along with me from Boston. He is supping with our late landlord (a Field-Marshal, at least, no doubt) in honour of our departure, and may be two hours longer. I walk again, but it gets duller and duller: the moon goes down: next June seems farther off in the dark, and the echoes of my footsteps make me nervous. It has turned cold too; and walking up and down without any companion in such lonely circumstances, is but poor amusement. So I break my stanch resolution, and think it may be, perhaps, as well to go to bed.

I go on board again; open the door of the gentleman's cabin, and walk in. Somehow or other – from its being so quiet I suppose – I have taken it into my head that there is nobody there. To my horror and amazement it is full of sleepers in every stage, shape, attitude, and variety of slumber: in the berths, on the chairs, on the floors, on the tables, and particularly round the stove, my detested enemy. I take another step forward, and slip upon the shining face of a black steward, who lies rolled in a blanket on the floor. He jumps up, grins, half in pain and half in hospitality; whispers my own name in my ear; and groping among the sleepers, leads me to my berth. Standing beside it, I count these slumbering passengers, and get past forty. There is no use in going farther, so I begin to undress. As the chairs are all occupied, and there is nothing else to put my clothes on, I deposite them upon the ground: not without soiling my hands, for it is in the same condition as the carpets in the Capitol, and from the same cause. Having but partially undressed, I clamber on my shelf, and hold the curtain open for a few minutes while I look round on all my fellow-travellers again. That done, I let it fall on them, and on the world: turn round, and go to sleep.

I wake, of course, when we get under weigh, for there is a good deal of noise. The day is then just breaking. Everybody / 163 wakes at the same time. Some are self-possessed directly, and some are much perplexed to make out where they are until they have rubbed their eyes, and, leaning on one elbow, look about them. Some yawn, some groan, nearly all spit, and a few get up. I am among the risers: for it is easy to feel, without going into the fresh air, that the atmosphere in the cabin is vile in the last degree. I huddle on my clothes, go down into the fore-cabin, get shaved by the barber, and wash myself. The washing and dressing apparatus for the passengers generally, consists of two jack towels, three small wooden basins, a keg of water and a ladle to serve it out with, six square inches of looking-glass, two ditto ditto of yellow soap, a comb and brush for the head, and nothing for the teeth. Everybody uses the comb and brush except myself. Everybody stares to see me using my own; and two or three gentlemen are strongly disposed to banter me on my prejudices, but don't. When I have made my toilet, I go upon the hurricane-deck, and set in for two hours of hard walking up and down. The sun is rising brilliantly, we are passing Mount Vernon, where Washington lies buried; the river is wide and rapid; and its banks are beautiful. All the glory and splendour of the day are coming on, and growing brighter every minute.

At eight o'clock, we breakfast in the cabin where I passed the night, but the windows and doors are all thrown open, and now it is fresh enough. There is no hurry or greediness apparent in the despatch of the meal. It is longer than a travelling breakfast with us; more orderly, and more polite.

Soon after nine o'clock we come to Potomac Creek, where we are to land: and then comes the oddest part of the journey. Seven stage-coaches are preparing to carry us on. Some of them are ready, some of them are not ready. Some of the drivers are blacks, some whites. There are four horses to each coach, and all the horses, harnessed or unharnessed, are there. The passengers are getting out of the steamboat, and into the coaches; the luggage is being transferred in noisy wheelbarrows, the horses are frightened, and impatient to start; the black drivers are chattering to them like so many / monkeys; and the white ones whooping like so many drovers; for the main thing to be done in all kinds of hostering here, is to make as much noise as possible. The coaches are something like the French coaches, but not nearly so good. In lieu of springs, they are hung on bands of the strongest leather. There is very little choice or difference between them; and they may be likened to the car portion of the swings at an English fair, roofed, put upon axletrees and wheels, and curtained with painted canvass. They are covered with mud from the roof to the wheel-tire, and have never been cleaned since they were first built.

164

The tickets we have received on board the steamboat are marked No. 1, so we belong to coach No. 1. I throw my coat on the box, and hoist my wife and her maid into the inside. It has only one step, and that being about a yard from the ground, is usually approached by a chair: when there is no chair, ladies trust in Providence. The coach holds nine inside, having a seat across from door to door, where we in England put our legs: so that there is only one feat more difficult in the performance than getting in, and that is, getting out again. There is only one outside passenger, and he sits upon the box. As I am that one, I climb up; and while they are strapping the luggage on the roof, and heaping it into a kind of tray behind, have a good opportunity of looking at the driver.

He is a negro – very black indeed. He is dressed in a coarse pepper-and-salt suit excessively patched and darned (particularly at the knees); gray stockings, enormous unblacked high-low shoes, and very short trousers. He has two odd gloves: one of parti-coloured worsted, and one of leather. He has a very short whip, broken in the middle and bandaged up with string. And yet he wears a low-crowned, broad-brimmed, black hat: faintly shadowing forth a kind of insane imitation of an English coachman! But somebody in authority cries "Go ahead!" as I am making these observations. The mail takes the lead in a four-horse wagon, and all the coaches follow in procession, headed by No. 1.

By-the-way, whenever an Englishman would cry "All right!" an American cries "Go ahead!" which is somewhat expressive of the national character of the two countries. . . .

Cincinnati

204 Cincinnati is a beautiful city; cheerful, thriving, and animated. I have not often seen a place that commends itself so favourably and pleasantly to a stranger at the first glance as this does: with its clean houses of red and white, its well-paved roads, and footways of bright tile. Nor does it become less prepossessing on a closer acquaintance. The streets are broad and airy, the shops extremely good, the private residences remarkable for their elegance and neatness. There is something of invention and fancy in the varying styles of these latter erections, which, after the dull company of the steamboat, is perfectly delightful, as conveying an assurance that there are such qualities still in existence. The disposition to ornament these pretty villas and render them attractive, leads to the culture of trees and flowers, and the laying out of well-kept gardens, the sight of which, to those who walk along the streets, is inexpressibly refreshing and agreeable. I was quite charmed with the appearance of the town, and its adjoining suburb of Mount Auburn; from which the city, lying in an amphitheatre of hills, forms a picture of remarkable beauty, and is seen to great advantage.

There happened to be a great Temperance Convention held here on the day after our arrival; and as the order of march brought the procession under the windows of the hotel in which we lodged, when they started in the morning, I had a good opportunity of seeing it. It comprised several thousand men; the members of various "Washington Auxiliary Temperance Societies;" and was marshalled by officers on horseback, who cantered briskly up and down the line, with scarves and ribands of bright colours fluttering out behind them gayly. There were bands of music, too, and banners out of number; and it was a fresh, holyday-looking concourse altogether.

I was particularly pleased to see the Irishmen, who formed a distinct society among themselves, and mustered very strong with their green scarves; carrying their national Harp and their Portrait of Father Mathew, high above the people's heads. They looked as jolly and good-humoured as ever; and, working the hardest for their living and doing any kind of sturdy labour that came in their way, were the most independent fellows there, I thought.

205 The banners were very well painted and flaunted down the street famously. There was the smiting of the rock, and the gushing forth of the waters; and there was a temperate man with "considerable of a hatchet" (as the standard-bearer would probably have said), aiming a deadly blow at a serpent which was apparently about to spring upon him from the top of a barrel of spirits. But the chief feature of this part of the show was a huge allegorical device, borne among the ship-carpenters, on one side whereof the steamboat Alcohol was represented bursting her boiler and exploding with a great crash, while upon the other, the good ship Temperance sailed away with a fair wind, to the heart's content of the captain, crew, and passengers.

After going round the town, the procession repaired to a certain appointed place, where, as the printed programme set forth, it would be received by the children of the different free-schools, "singing Temperance Songs." I was prevented from getting there, in time to hear these Little Warblers, or to report upon this novel kind of vocal entertainment: novel, at least, to me: but I found, in a large open space, each society gathered round its own banners, and listening in silent attention to its own orator. The speeches, judging from the little I could hear of them, were certainly adapted to the occasion, as having that degree of relationship to cold water which wet blankets may claim: but the main thing was the conduct and appearance of the audience throughout the day; and that was admirable and full of promise.

Cincinnati is honourably famous for its free-schools, of which it has so many that no person's child among its population can, by possibility, want the means of education, which are extended, upon an average, to four thousand pupils, annually. I was only present in one of these establishments during the hours of instruction. In the boys' department, which was full of little urchins (varying in their ages, I should say, from six years old to ten or twelve), the master offered to institute an extemporary examination of the pupils in algebra; a proposal, which, as I was by no means confident of 206 my ability to detect / mistakes in that science, I declined with some alarm. In the girls' school, reading was proposed, and as I felt tolerably equal to that art, I expressed my willingness to hear a class. – Books were distributed accordingly, and some half dozen girls relieved each other in reading paragraphs from English History. But it was a dry compilation, infinitely above their powers; and when they had blundered through three or four dreary passages concerning the Treaty of Amiens, and other thrilling topics of the same nature (obviously without comprehending ten words), I expressed myself quite satisfied. It is very possible that they only mounted to this exalted stave in the Ladder of Learning, for the astonishment of a visiter; and that at other times they keep upon its lower rounds; but I should have been much better pleased and satisfied if I had heard them exercised in simpler lessons, which they understood.

As in every other place I visited, the Judges here were gentlemen of high character and attainments. I was in one of the courts for a few minutes, and found it like those to which I have already referred. A nuisance cause was trying; there were not many spectators; and the witnesses, counsel, and jury, formed a sort of family circle, sufficiently jocose and snug.

The society with which I mingled, was intelligent, courteous, and agreeable. The inhabitants of Cincinnati are proud of their city, as one of the most interesting in America: and with reason: for beautiful and thriving as it is now, and containing, as it does, a population of fifty thousand souls, but two-and-fifty years have passed away since the ground on which it stands (bought at that time for a few dollars) was a wild wood, and its citizens were but a handful of dwellers in scattered log huts upon the river's shore. . . .

Slavery

291 The upholders of slavery in America – of the atrocities of which system, I shall not write one word for which I have not ample proof and warrant – may be divided into three great classes.

The first, are those more moderate and rational owners of human cattle, who have come into the possession of them as so many coins in their trading capital, but who admit the frightful nature of the Institution in the abstract, and perceive the dangers to society with which it is fraught, dangers which, however distant they may be, or howsoever tardy in their coming on, are as certain to fall upon its guilty head, as is the Day of Judgment.

The second, consists of all those owners, breeders, users, buyers, and sellers of slaves, who will, until the bloody chapter has a bloody end, own, breed, use, buy, and sell them at all hazards; who doggedly deny the horrors of the system, in the teeth of such a mass of evidence as never was brought to bear on any other subject, and to which the experience of every day contributes its immense amount; who would at this or any other moment, gladly involve America in a war, civil or foreign, provided that it had, for its sole end and object the assertion of their right to perpetuate slavery, and to whip, and work, and torture slaves, unquestioned by any human authority, and unassailed by any human power; who, when 292 they speak of / Freedom, mean the Freedom to oppress their kind, and to be savage, merciless, and cruel; and of whom every man on his own ground, in republican America, is a more exacting, and a sterner and less responsible despot, than the Caliph Haroun Alraschid in his angry robe of scarlet.

The third, and not the least numerous or influential, is composed of all that delicate gentility which cannot bear a superior, and cannot brook an equal: of that class whose Republicanism means, "I will not tolerate a man above me; and of those below, none must approach too near;" whose pride, in a land where voluntary servitude is shunned as a disgrace, must be ministered to by slaves; and whose inalienable rights can only have their growth in negro wrongs.

It has been sometimes urged that, in the unavailing efforts which have been made to advance the cause of Human Freedom in the republic of America (strange cause for history to treat of!), sufficient regard has not been had to the existence of the first class of persons; and it has been contended that they are hardly used, in being confounded with the second. This is, no doubt, the case; noble instances of pecuniary and personal sacrifice have already had their growth among them; and it is much to be regretted that the gulf between them and the advocates of emancipation should have been widened and deepened by any means: the rather, as there are, beyond dispute, among these slave-owners, many kind masters who are tender in the exercise of their unnatural power. Still it is to be feared that this injustice is inseparable from the state of things with which humanity and truth are called upon to deal. Slavery is not a whit the more endurable because some hearts are to be found which can partially resist its hardening influences; nor can the indignant tide of honest wrath stand still, because in its onward course it overwhelms a few who are comparatively innocent, among a host of guilty.

The ground most commonly taken by these better men among the advocates of slavery, is this: "It is a bad system; and for myself I would willingly get rid of it, if I could; most willingly. But it is not so bad, as you in England take it to be. You are / deceived by the representations of the 293 emancipationists. The greater part of my slaves are much attached to me. You will say that I do not allow them to be severely treated; but I will put it to you whether you believe that it can be a general practice to treat them inhumanly, when it would impair their value, and would be obviously against the interests of their masters."

Is it the interest of any man to steal, to game, to waste his health and mental faculties by drunkenness, to lie, forswear himself, indulge hatred, seek desperate revenge, or do murder? No. All these are roads to ruin. And why, then, do men tread them? Because such inclinations are among the vicious qualities of mankind. Blot out, ye friends of slavery, from the catalogue of human passions, brutal lust, cruelty, and the abuse of irresponsible power (of all earthly temptations the most difficult to be resisted), and when ye have done so, and not before, we will inquire whether it be the interest of a master to lash and maim the slaves, over whose lives and limbs he has an absolute control. . . .

Concluding Remarks

311 There are many passages in this book, where I have been at some pains to resist the temptation of troubling my readers with my own deductions and conclusions; preferring that they should judge for themselves, from such premises as I have laid before them. My only object in the outset, was, to carry them with me faithfully wheresoever I went, and that task I have discharged.

But I may be pardoned, if on such a theme as the general character of the American people, and the general character of their social system, as presented to a stranger's eyes, I desire to express my own opinions in a few words, before I bring the volume to a close.

They are, by nature, frank, brave, cordial, hospitable, and affectionate. Cultivation and refinement seem but to enhance their warmth of heart and ardent enthusiasm; and it is the possession of these latter qualities in a most remarkable degree, which renders an educated American one of the most endearing and most generous of friends. I never was so won upon, as by this class; never yielded up my full confidence and esteem so readily and pleasurably, as to them; never can make again, in half a year, so many friends for whom I seem to entertain the regard of half a life.

These qualities are natural, I implicitly believe, to the whole people. That they are, 312 however, sadly sapped and blighted / in their growth among the mass; and that there are influences at work which endanger them still more, and give but little present promise of their healthy restoration; is a truth that ought to be told.

It is an essential part of every national character to pique itself mightily upon its faults, and to deduce tokens of its virtue or its wisdom from their very exaggeration. One great blemish in the popular mind of America, and the prolific parent of an innumerable brood of evils, is Universal Distrust. Yet, the American citizen plumes himself upon this spirit, even when he is sufficiently dispassionate to perceive the ruin it works; and will often adduce it, in spite of his own reason, as an instance of the great sagacity and acuteness of the people, and their superior shrewdness and independence.

"You carry," says the stranger, "this jealousy and distrust into every transaction of public life. By repelling worthy men from your legislative assemblies, it has bred up a class of candidates for the suffrage, who, in their every act, disgrace your Institutions and your people's choice. It has rendered you so fickle, and so given to change, that your inconstancy has passed into a proverb, for you no sooner set up an idol firmly, than you are sure to pull it down and dash it into fragments; and this, because directly you reward a benefactor, or a public servant, you distrust him, merely because he *is* rewarded; and immediately apply yourselves to find out, either that you have been too bountiful in your acknowledgements, or he remiss in his deserts. Any man who attains a high place among you, from the President downward, may date his downfall from that moment; for any printed lie that any notorious villain pens, although it militate directly against the character and conduct of a life, appeals at once to your distrust, and is believed. You will strain at a gnat in the way of trustfulness and confidence, however fairly won and well deserved; but you will swallow a whole caravan of camels, if they be laden with unworthy doubts and mean suspicions. Is this well, think you, or likely to elevate the character of the governors or the governed among you?"

The answer is invariably the same: 313 "There's freedom of opinion here, you know. Every man thinks for himself, and we are not to be easily overreached. That's how our people come to be suspicious."

Another prominent feature is the love of "smart" dealing, which gilds over many a swindle and gross breach of trust; many a defalcation, public and private; and enables many a knave to hold his head up with the best, who well deserves a halter – though it has not been without its retributive operation, for this smartness has done more in a few years to impair the public credit, and to cripple the public resources, than dull honesty, however rash, could have effected in a century. The merits of a broken speculation, or a bankruptcy, or of a successful scoundrel, are not gauged by its or his observance of the golden rule, "Do as you would be done by," but are considered with reference to their smartness. I recollect, on both occasions of our passing that ill-fated Cairo on the Mississippi, remarking on the bad effects such gross deceits must have when they exploded, in generating a want of confidence abroad, and discouraging foreign investment; but I was given to understand that this was a very smart scheme by which a deal of money had been made; and that its smartest feature was, that they forgot these things abroad in a very short time, and speculated again as freely as ever. The following dialogue I have held a hundred times: "Is it not a very disgraceful circumstance that such a man as So-and-so should be acquiring a large property by the most infamous and odious means, and, notwithstanding all the crimes of which he has been guilty, should be tolerated and abetted by your citizens? He is a public nuisance, is he not?" "Yes, sir." "A convicted liar?" "Yes, sir." "He has been kicked, and cuffed, and caned?" "Yes, sir." "And he is utterly dishonourable, debased, and profligate?" "Yes, sir." "In the name of wonder, then, what is his merit?" "Well, sir, he is a smart man."

In like manner, all kinds of deficient and impolitic usages are referred to the national love of trade; though, oddly enough, it would be a weighty charge against a foreigner, that he 314 / regarded the Americans as a trading people. The love of trade is assigned as a reason for that comfortless custom, so very prevalent in country towns, of married persons living in hotels, having no fireside of their own, and seldom meeting from early morning until late at night, but at the hasty public meals. The love of trade is a reason why the literature of America is to remain forever unprotected: "For we are a trading people, and don't care for poetry," though we *do,* by-the-way, profess to be very proud of our poets; while healthful amusements, cheerful means of recreation, and wholesome fancies, must fade before the stern utilitarian joys of trade.

These three characteristics are strongly presented at every turn, full in the stranger's view. But the foul growth of America has a more tangled root than this, and it strikes its fibres deep in its licentious Press.

Schools may be erected East, West, North, and South; pupils be taught, and masters reared, by scores upon scores of thousands; colleges may thrive, churches may be crammed, temperance may be diffused, and advancing knowledge in all other forms walk through the land with giant strides; but, while the newspaper press of America is in, or near, its present abject state, high moral improvement in that country is hopeless. Year by year it must and will go back; year by year the tone of public feeling must sink lower down; year by year the Congress and the Senate must become of less account before all decent men; and, year by year, the memory of the Great Fathers of the Revolution must be outraged more and more in the bad life of their degenerate child.

Among the herd of journals which are published in the States, there are some, the reader scarcely need be told, of character and credit. From personal intercourse with accomplished gentlemen connected with publications of this class I have derived both pleasure and profit. But the name of these is Few, and of the others Legion; and the influence of the good is powerless to counteract the mortal poison of the bad.

Among the gentry of America; among the well-informed and moderate; in the learned professions; at the bar and on the / bench, 315 there is, as there can be, but one opinion in reference to the vicious character of these infamous journals. It is sometimes contended – I will not say strangely, for it is natural to seek excuses for such a disgrace –

that their influence is not so great as a visiter would suppose. I must be pardoned for saying that there is no warrant for this plea, and that every fact and circumstance tends directly to the opposite conclusion.

When any man, of any grade of desert in intellect or character, can climb to any public distinction, no matter what, in America, without first grovelling down upon the earth, and bending the knee before this monster of depravity; when any private excellence is safe from its attacks, and when any social confidence is left unbroken by it, or any tie of social decency and honour is held in the least regard; when any man in that Free Country has freedom of opinion, and presumes to think for himself, and speak for himself, without humble reference to a censorship which, for its rampant ignorance and base dishonesty, he utterly loathes and despises in his heart; when those who most acutely feel its infamy and the reproach it casts upon the nation, and who most denounce it to each other, dare to set their heels upon and crush it openly, in the sight of all men; then, I will believe that its influence is lessening, and men are returning to their manly senses. But while that Press has its evil eye in every house, and its black hand in every appointment in the state, from a president to a postman; while, with ribald slander for its only stock in trade, it is the standard literature of an enormous class, who must find their reading in a newspaper, or they will not read at all; so long must its odium be upon the country's head, and so long must the evil it works, be plainly visible in the Republic.

To those who are accustomed to the leading English Journals, or to the respectable journals of the Continent of Europe; to those who are accustomed to anything else in print and paper; it would be impossible, without an amount of extract for which I have neither space nor inclination, to convey an adequate idea of this frightful engine in America. But if any man desire confirmation of my statement on this head, 316 let him repair to / any place in this city of London where scattered numbers of these publications are to be found; and there let him form his own opinion.*

It would be well, there can be no doubt, for the American people as a whole, if they loved the Real less, and the Ideal somewhat more. It would be well, if there were greater encouragement to lightness of heart and gayety, and a wider cultivation of what is beautiful, without being eminently and directly useful. But then, I think the general remonstrance, "we are a new country," which is so often advanced as an excuse for defects which are quite unjustifiable, as being, of right, only the slow growth of an old one, may be very reasonably urged; and I yet hope to hear of there being some other national amusement in the United States, besides newspaper politics.

They certainly are not a humorous people, and their temperament always impressed me as being of a dull and gloomy character. In shrewdness of remark, and a certain cast-iron quaintness, the Yankees, or people of New-England, unquestionably take the lead; as they do in most other evidences of intelligence. But in travelling about, out of the large cities, as I have remarked in former parts of this volume; I was quite oppressed by the prevailing seriousness and melancholy air of business: which was so general and unvarying, that at every new town I came to, I seemed to meet the very same people whom I had left behind me, at the last. Such defects as are perceptibly in the national manners, seem, to me, to be referable, in a great degree, to this cause: which has generated a dull, sullen persistence in coarse usages, and rejected the graces of life as undeserving of attention. There is no doubt that Washington, who was always most scrupulous and exact on points of ceremony, perceived the

* Or, let him refer to an able, and perfectly truthful article, in *The Foreign Quarterly Review,* published in the present month of October; to which my attention has been attracted, since these sheets have been passing through the press. He will find some specimens there, by no means remarkable to any man who has been in America, but sufficiently striking to one who has not. [Note by Dickens]

tendency towards this mistake, even in his time; and did his utmost to correct it.

317 I cannot hold with other writers on these subjects that the prevalence of various forms of dissent in America, is in any way attributable to the non-existence there, of an established church: indeed, I think the temper of the people, if it admitted of such an Institution being founded among them, would lead them to desert it, as a matter of course, merely because it was established. But, supposing it to exist, I doubt its probable efficacy in summoning the wandering sheep to one great fold, simply because of the immense amount of dissent which prevails at home: and because I do not find in America any one form of religion with which we in Europe, or even in England, are unacquainted. Dissenters resort thither in great numbers, as other people do, simply because it is a land of resort: and great settlements of them are founded, because ground can be purchased, and towns and villages reared, where there were none of the human creation before. But even the Shakers emigrated from England: our country is not unknown to Mr. Joseph Smith, the apostle of Mormonism, or to his benighted disciples: I have beheld religious scenes myself in some of our populous towns which can hardly be surpassed by an American camp-meeting; and I am not aware that any instance of superstitious imposture on the one hand, and superstitious credulity on the other, has had its origin in the United States, which we cannot more than parallel by the precedents of Mrs. Southcote, Mary Tofts, the rabbit-breeder, or even Mr. Thom of Canterbury: which latter case arose, some time after the dark ages had passed away.

The Republican Institutions of America undoubtedly lead the people to assert their self-respect and their equality; but a traveller is bound to bear those Institutions in his mind, and not hastily to resent the near approach of a class of strangers, who, at home, would keep aloof. This characteristic, when it was tinctured with no foolish pride, and stopped short of no honest service, never offended me: and I very seldom, if ever, experienced its rude or unbecoming display. Once or twice it was comically developed, as in the following case: but this was an amusing incident, and not the rule nor near it.

318 I wanted a pair of boots at a certain town, for I had none to travel in, but those with the memorable cork soles, which were much too hot for the fiery decks of a steamboat. I therefore sent a message to an artist in boots, importing, with my compliments, that I should be happy to see him, if he would do me the polite favour to call. He very kindly returned for answer that he would "look round" at six o'clock that evening.

I was lying on the sofa, with a book and a wineglass, at about that time, when the door opened, and a gentleman in a stiff cravat, within a year or two on either side of thirty, entered, in his hat and gloves; walked up to the looking-glass; arranged his hair; took off his gloves; slowly produced a measure from the uttermost depths of his coat-pocket; and requested me, in a languid tone, to "unfix" my straps. I complied, but looked with some curiosity at his hat, which was still upon his head. It might have been that, or it might have been the heat—but he took it off. Then he sat himself down on a chair opposite to me; rested an arm on each knee; and, leaning forward very much, took from the ground, by a great effort, the specimen of metropolitan workmanship which I had just pulled off—whistling, pleasantly, as he did so. He turned it over and over; surveyed it with a contempt no language can express; and inquired if I wished him to fix me a boot like *that?* I courteously replied, that provided the boots were large enough, I would leave the rest to him; that if convenient and practicable, I should not object to their bearing some resemblance to the model then before him; but that I would be entirely guided by, and would beg to leave the whole subject to his judgment and discretion. "You an't partickler about this scoop in the heel, I suppose then?" says he: "we don't foller that, here." I repeated my last observation. He looked at himself in the glass again; went closer to it to dash a grain or two of dust out of the corner of his eye; and settled his cravat. All this time, my leg and foot were in the air. "Nearly ready, sir?" I inquired. "Well, pretty nigh," he said; "keep steady." 319 I kept as steady / as I could, both in foot and face; and having by this time got the dust out, and found his pencil-case, he measured me, and made the necessary notes. When he had finished, he fell into his old attitude, and taking up the boot again, mused for some time. "And this," he said, at last, "is an English boot, is it? This is a London boot, eh?" "That, sir," I replied, "is a London boot." He mused over it again, after the manner of Hamlet with Yorick's scull; nodded his head, as who should say "I pity the institutions that led to the production of this boot!" rose; put up his pencil, notes, and paper – glancing at himself in the glass, all the time – put on his hat, drew on his gloves very slowly, and finally walked out. When he had been gone about a minute, the door reopened, and his hat and his head reappeared. He looked round the room, and at the boot again, which was still lying on the floor; appeared thoughtful for a minute; and then said, "Well, good arternoon." "Good afternoon, sir," said I; and that was the end of the interview.

There is but one other head on which I wish to offer a remark: and that has reference to the public health. In so vast a country, where there are thousands of millions of acres of land yet unsettled and uncleared, and on every rood of which, vegetable decomposition is annually taking place; where there are so many great rivers, and such opposite varieties of climate; there cannot fail to be a great amount of sickness at certain seasons. But I may venture to say, after conversing with many members of the medical profession in America, that I am not singular in the opinion that much of the disease which does prevail, might be avoided, if a few common precautions were observed. Greater means of personal cleanliness are indispensable to this end; the custom of hastily swallowing large quantities of animal food, three times a day, and rushing back to sedentary pursuits after each meal, must be changed; the gentler sex must go more wisely clad, and take more healthy exercise; and in the latter clause, the males must be included also. Above all, in public institutions, and throughout the whole of every town and city, the system of / ventilation, and drainage, and removal 320 of impurities, requires to be thoroughly revised. There is no local legislature in America which may not study Mr. Chadwick's excellent Report upon the Sanitary condition of our Labouring Classes, with immense advantage.

I have now arrived at the close of this book. I have little reason to believe, from certain warnings I have had since I returned to England, that it will be tenderly or favourably received by the American people; and as I have written the truth in relation to the mass of those who form their judgment and express their opinions, it will be seen that I have no desire to court, by any adventitious means, the popular applause.

It is enough for me to know, that what I have set down in these pages, cannot cost me a single friend on the other side of the Atlantic, who is, in anything, deserving of the name. For the rest, I put my trust implicitly in the spirit in which they have been conceived and penned, and I can bide my time.

I have made no reference to my reception, nor have I suffered it to influence me in what I have written; for, in either case, I should have offered but a sorry acknowledgment, compared with that I bear within my breast, towards those partial readers of my former books across the water, who met me with an open hand, and not with one that closed upon an iron muzzle.

Alexis de Tocqueville

From *Democracy in America* by Alexis de Tocqueville. Translated by Henry Reeve. Two volumes. New York (George Adlard), 1838.

Born in Paris, educated as an aristocrat, and trained in the law, Alexis de Tocqueville was a young apprentice magistrate in France when, in 1831, he was sent to the United States by his government to examine the new nation's penal system and its progress in prison reform. However, De Tocqueville's real interests were much broader than American prisons. When he returned to France he brought out the first two of four volumes called *Democracy in America* (1835), a classic analysis of the influence of democracy on the government, the economy, and the society of the United States. De Tocqueville's study was acclaimed in France, the young writer was welcomed into the intellectual circles of his day, and he was shortly elected to the French Academy. He continued for some time in public life rising to vice-presidency of the assembly and then, briefly, minister of foreign affairs, but he withdrew from politics in disgust with the triumph of Louis Napoleon. Never very robust, he died in Cannes in his mid-fifties. More than any other visitor to America in the Jacksonian era De Tocqueville was concerned with how our Democratic machinery actually functioned and what were its implications for Europe, particularly for France. The selections here included — as is true of virtually all of his work — demonstrate De Tocqueville's skill in searching out and exposing the subtle and intricate ramifications of the democratic principle in American society.

[The Negro in the United States]

I, 314 The Negro has no family: woman is merely the temporary companion of his pleasures, and his children are on an equality with himself from the moment of their birth. Am I to call it a proof of God's mercy or a visitation of his wrath, that man, in certain states appears to be insensible to his extreme wretchedness and almost obtains a depraved taste, for the cause of his misfortunes? The Negro, who is plunged in this abyss of evils, scarcely feels his own calamitous situation. Violence made him a slave, and the habit of servitude gives him the thoughts and desires of a slave; he admires his tyrants more than he hates them, and finds his joy and his pride in the servile imitation of those who oppress him. His understanding is degraded to the level of his soul.

The Negro enters upon slavery as soon as he is born; nay, he may have been purchased in the womb, and have begun his slavery before he began his existence. Equally devoid of wants and of enjoyment, and useless to himself, he learns, with his first notions of existence, that he is the property of another, who has an interest in preserving his life, and that the care of it does not devolve upon himself; even the power of thought appears to him a useless gift of Providence, and he quietly enjoys the privileges of his debasement. If he becomes free, independence is often felt by him to be a heavier burden than slavery; for, having learned in the course of his life to submit to everything except reason, he is too much unacquainted with her dictates to obey them. A thousand new desires beset him, and he is destitute of the knowledge and energy necessary to resist them: these are masters which it is necessary to contend with, and he has learnt only to submit and obey. In short, he sinks to such a depth of wretchedness, that while servitude brutalizes, liberty destroys him. . . .

I see that in a certain portion of the I, 339

territory of the United States at the present day, the legal barrier which separated the two races is tending to fall away, but not that which exists in the manners of the country; slavery recedes, but the prejudice to which it has given birth remains stationary. Whosoever has inhabited the United States must have perceived that in those parts of the Union in which the Negroes are no longer slaves, they have in nowise drawn nearer to the whites. On the contrary, the prejudice of the race appears to be stronger in the States which have abolished slavery, than in those where it still exists; and nowhere is it so intolerant as in those States where servitude has never been known.

It is true, that in the North of the Union, marriages may be legally contracted between Negroes and whites; but public opinon would stigmatize as infamous a man who should connect himself with a Negress, and it would be difficult to meet with a single instance of such a union. The electoral franchise has been conferred upon the Negroes in almost all the states in which slavery has been abolished; but if they come forward to vote, their lives are in danger. If oppressed, they may bring an action at law, but they will find none but whites among their judges; and although they may I, 340 legally serve as jurors, prejudice repulses / them from that office. The same schools do not receive the children of the black and of the European. In the theaters, gold cannot procure a seat for the servile race beside their former masters; in the hospitals they lie apart; and although they are allowed to invoke the same Divinity as the whites, it must be at a different altar and in their own churches, with their own clergy. The gates of Heaven are not closed against these unhappy beings; but their inferiority is continued to the very confines of the other world. When the Negro is defunct, his bones are cast aside, and the distinction of condition prevails even in the equality of death. The Negro is free, but he can share neither the rights, nor the pleasures, nor the labor, nor the afflictions, nor the tomb of him whose equal he has been declared to be; and he cannot meet him upon fair terms in life or in death.

In the South, where slavery still exists, the Negroes are less carefully kept apart; they sometimes share the labors and the recreations of the whites; the whites consent to intermix with them to a certain extent, and although the legislation treats them more harshly, the habits of the people are more tolerant and compassionate. In the South the master is not afraid to raise his slave to his own standing, because he knows that he can in a moment reduce him to the dust at pleasure. In the North the white no longer distinctly perceives the barrier that separates him from the degraded race, and he shuns the Negro with the more pertinacity since he fears lest they should some day be confounded together. . . .

Thus it is in the United States that the prejudice which repels the Negroes seems to increase in proportion as they are emancipated, and inequality is sanctioned by the manners whilst it is effaced from the laws of the country. . . .

I, 359 When I contemplate the condition of the South, I can only discover two alternatives which may be adopted by the white inhabitants of those States; viz. either to emancipate the Negroes and to intermingle with them, or, remaining isolated from them, to keep them in slavery as long as possible. All intermediate measures seem to me likely to terminate, and that shortly, in the most horrible of civil wars and perhaps in the extirpation of one or the other of the two races. Such is the view which the Americans of the South take of the question, and they act consistently with it. As they are determined not to mingle with the Negroes, they refuse to emancipate them.

Not that the inhabitants of the South regard slavery as necessary to the wealth of the planter; for on this point many of them agree with their Northern countrymen in freely admitting that slavery is prejudicial to their interests; but they are convinced that, they hold their lives upon no other tenure. The instruction which is now diffused in the South has convinced the inhabitants that slavery is injurious to the slave-owner, but it has also shown them, more clearly than before, that it is almost an impossibility to get rid of its bad consequences. Hence arises a singular contrast; the more the utility of slavery is contested, the more firmly is it established in the laws; and while its principle is gradually abolished in the North, that selfsame principle gives rise to more and more rigorous consequences in the South. . . .

I, 361 Whatever may be the efforts of the Americans of the South to maintain slavery, they will not always succeed. Slavery, which is now confined to a single tract of the civilized earth, attacked by Christianity as unjust and by political economy as prejudicial, and which is now contrasted with democratic liberties and the intelligence of our age, cannot survive. By the choice of the master, or by the will of the slave, it will cease; and in either case great calamities may be expected to ensue. If liberty be refused to the Negroes of the South, they will in the end forcibly seize it for themselves; if it be given, they will abuse it ere long. . . .

[President Jackson]

I, 392 Almost all the controversies of which I have been speaking have taken place under the Presidency of General Jackson; and it cannot be denied that in the question of the Tariff he has supported the claims of the Union with energy and skill. I think, however, that the conduct of this President of the Federal government may be reckoned as one of the dangers which threaten its continuance.

Some persons in Europe have formed an opinion of the possible influence of General Jackson upon the affairs of his country which appears highly extravagant to those who have seen the subject nearer at hand. We have been told that General Jackson has won sundry battles; that he is an energetic man, prone by nature and habit to the use of force, covetous of power, and a despot by taste. All this may be true; but the inferences which have been drawn from these truths are very erroneous. It has been imagined that General Jackson is bent / on (I, 393) establishing a dictatorship in America, on introducing a military spirit, and giving a degree of influence to the central authority that cannot but be dangerous to provincial liberties. But in America the time for similar undertakings, and the age for men of this kind, has not yet come: if General Jackson had entertained a hope of exercising his authority in this manner, he would infallibly have forfeited his political station, and compromised his life; accordingly he has not been so imprudent as to make any such attempt.

Far from wishing to extend the Federal power, the President belongs to the party which is desirous of limiting that power to the clear and precise letter of the Constitution, and which never puts a construction upon that act favorable to the government of the Union; far from standing forth as the champion of centralization; General Jackson is the agent of all the jealousies of the States; and he was placed in his lofty station by the passions of the people which are most opposed to the central Government. It is by perpetually flattering these passions, that he maintains his station and his popularity. General Jackson is the slave of the majority: he yields to its wishes, its propensities, and its demands — say, rather, anticipates and forestalls them.

Whenever the governments of the states come into collision with that of the Union, the President is generally the first to question his own rights; he almost always outstrips the legislature; and when the extent of the Federal power is controverted, he takes part, as it were, against himself; he conceals his official interests, and labors to diminish his own dignity. Not, indeed, that he is naturally weak or hostile to the Union; for when the majority decided against the claims of nullification, he put himself at their head, asserted distinctly and energetically the doctrines which the nation held, and was the first to recommend force; but General Jackson appears to me, if I may use the American expression, to be a Federalist by taste and a Republican by calculation.

General Jackson stoops to gain the favor of the majority; but when he feels that his popularity is secure, he overthrows all obstacles in the pursuit of the objects which the community approves or of those which it does not regard with a jealous eye. He is supported by a power which his predecessors never had, he tramples on his personal enemies, whenever they cross his path, with a facility without example; he takes upon himself the responsibility of measures that no one before him would have ventured to attempt; he even treats the national representatives with a disdain approaching to insult; he puts his Veto up on the laws of Congress and frequently neglects even to reply to that powerful body. He is a favorite who sometimes treats his master roughly. The power of General Jackson perpetually increases, but that of the President declines; in his hands the Federal government is strong, but it will pass enfeebled into the hands of his successor. . . .

[Literature in the United States]

II, 57 When a traveller goes into a bookseller's shop in the United States, and examines the American books upon the shelves, the number of works appears extremely great; while that of known authors appears, on the contrary to be extremely small. He will first meet with a number of elementary treatises, destined to teach the rudiments of human knowledge. Most of these books are written in Europe; the Americans reprint them, adapting them to their own country. Next comes an enormous quantity of religious works, Bibles, sermons, edifiyng anecdotes, controversial divinity, and reports of charitable societies; lastly, appears the long catalogue of political pamphlets. In America, parties do not write books to combat each others' opinions, but pamphlets which are circulated for a day with incredible rapidity, and then expire.

In the midst of all these obscure productions of the human brain are to be found the more remarkable works of that small number of authors whose names are, or ought to be, known to Europeans.

Although America is perhaps in our days the civilized country in which literature is least attended to, a large number of persons are nevertheless to be found there who take an interest in the productions of the mind, and who make them, if not the study of their lives, at least the charm of their leisure hours. But England supplies these readers with the larger portion of the books which they require. Almost all important English books are republished in the United States. The literary genius of Great Britain still darts its rays into the recesses of the forests of the New World. There is hardly a pioneer's hut which does not contain a few odd volumes of Shakespeare. I remember that I read the feudal play of Henry V for the first time in a log-house.

II, 58 Not only do the Americans constantly draw upon the treasures of English literature, but it may be said with truth that they find the literature of England growing on their own soil. The larger part of that small number of men in the United States who are engaged in the composition of literary works are English in substance, and still more so in form. Thus they transport into the midst of democracy the ideas and literary fashions which are current among the aristocratic nation they have taken for their model. They paint with colours borrowed from foreign manners; and as they hardly ever represent the country they were born in as it really is, they are seldom popular there.

The citizens of the United States are themselves so convinced that it is not for them that books are published, that before they can make up their minds upon the merit of one of their authors they generally wait till his fame has been ratified in England, just as in pictures the author of an original is held to be entitled to judge of the merit of a copy. . . .

II, 63 Democracy not only infuses a taste for letters among the trading classes, but introduces a trading spirit into literature.

In aristocracies, readers are fastidious and few in number; in democracies, they are far more numerous and far less difficult to please. The consequence is, that among aristocratic nations no one can hope to succeed without immense exertions, and that these exertions may bestow a great deal of fame, but never can earn much money; while among democratic nations, a writer may flatter himself that he will obtain at a cheap rate a meager reputation and a large fortune. For this purpose he need not be admired; it is enough that he is liked.

The ever-increasing crowd of readers, and their continual craving for something new, insures the sale of books which nobody much esteems.

In democratic periods the public frequently treat authors as kings do their courtiers; they enrich, and they despise them. What more is needed by the venal souls which are born in courts, or which are worthy to live there?

Democratic literature is always infested with a tribe of writers who look upon letters as a mere trade; and for some few great authors who adorn it, you may reckon thousands of idea-mongers. . . .

II, 78 I readily admit that the Americans have no poets; I cannot allow that they have no poetic ideas. In Europe people talk a great deal of the wilds of America, but the Americans themselves never think about them: they are insensible to the wonders of inanimate nature, and they may be said not to perceive the mighty forests which surround them till they fall beneath the hatchet. Their eyes are fixed upon another sight: the American people views its own march across these wilds – drying swamps, turning the course of rivers, peopling solitudes, and subduing nature. This magnificent image of themselves does not meet the gaze of the Americans at intervals only; it may be said to haunt every one of them in his least as well as in his most important actions, and to be always flitting before his mind. Nothing conceivable is so petty, so insipid, so crowded with paltry interests, in one word so anti-poetic, as the life of a man in the United States. But among the thoughts which it suggests there is always one which is full of poetry, and that is the hidden nerve which gives vigor to the frame. . . .

[Sunday in the United States]

II, 152 In the United States, on the seventh day of every week, the trading and working life of the nation seems suspended; all noises cease; a deep tranquility, say rather the solemn calm of meditation, succeeds the turmoil of the week, and the soul resumes possession and contemplation of itself. Upon this day the marts of traffic are deserted; every member of the community, accompanied by his children, goes to church, where he listens to strange language which would seem unsuited to his ear. He is told of the countless evils caused by pride and covetousness: he is reminded of the necessity of checking his desires, of the finer pleasures that belong to virtue alone, and of the true happiness which attends it. On his return home, he does not turn to the ledgers of his calling, but he opens the book of Holy Scripture; there he meets with sublime or affecting descriptions of the greatness and goodness of the Creator, of the infinite magnificence of the handiwork of God, of the lofty destinies of man, of his duties, and of his immortal privileges.

Thus it is that the American at times steals an hour from himself; and laying aside for a while the petty passions which agitate his life, and the ephemeral interests which engross it, he strays at once into an ideal world, where all is great, eternal, and pure. . . .

[Democracy, Masters, and Servants]

II, 190 Equality of conditions turns servants and masters into new beings, and places them in new relative positions. When social conditions are nearly equal, men are constantly changing their situations in life: there is still a class of menials and a class of masters, but these classes are not always composed of the same individuals, still less of the same families; and those who command are not / II, 191 more secure of perpetuity than those who obey. As servants do not form a separate people, they have no habits, prejudices, or manners peculiar to themselves: they are not remarkable for any particular turn of mind or moods of feeling. They know no vices or virtues of their condition, but they partake of the education, the opinions, the feelings, the virtues and the vices of their contemporaries; and they are honest men or scoundrels in the same way as their masters are.

The conditions of servants are not less equal than those of masters. As no marked ranks or fixed subordination are to be found among them, they will not display either the meanness or the greatness which characterize the aristocracy of menials as well as all other aristocracies. I never saw a man in the United States who reminded me of that class of confidential servants of which we still retain a reminiscence in Europe, neither did I ever meet with such a thing as a lacquey: all traces of the one and of the other have disappeared. . . .

II, 193 I would fain illustrate these reflections [on relationships of servants and masters] by the example of the Americans; but for this purpose the distinctions of persons and places must be accurately traced.

In the south of the Union, slavery exists; all that I have just said is consequently inapplicable there. In the north, the majority of servants are either freed-men or the children of freed-men; these persons occupy a contested position in the public estimation; by the laws they are brought up to the level of their masters — by the manners of the country they are obstinately detruded from it. They do not themselves clearly know their proper place, and they are almost always either insolent or craven.

But in the northern States, especially in New England, there are a certain number of whites, who agree, for wages, to yield a temporary obedience to the will of their fellow-citizens. I have heard that these servants commonly perform the duties of their situation with punctuality and intelligence; and that, without thinking themselves naturally inferior to the person who orders them, they submit without reluctance to obey him.

They appear to me to carry into service some of those manly habits which independence and equality engender. Having once selected a hard way of life, they do not seek to escape from it by indirect means; and they have sufficient respect for themselves not to refuse to their masters that obedience which they have freely promised.

On their part, masters require nothing of their servants but the faithful and rigorous performance of the covenant: they do not ask for marks of respect, they do not claim their love or devoted attachment; it is enough that, as servants, they are exact and honest.

It would not then be true to assert that, in democratic society, the relation of servants and masters is disorganized: it is organized on another footing; the rule is different, but there is a rule. . . .

II, 194 In democracies the condition of domestic service does not degrade the character of those who enter upon it, because it is freely chosen, and adopted for a time only; because it is not stigmatized by public opinion, and creates no permanent inequality between the servant and the master. . . .

[Young Women in the United States]

II, 209 Long before an American girl arrives at the age of marriage, her emancipation from maternal control begins: she has scarcely ceased to be a child when she already thinks for herself, speaks with freedom, and acts on her own impulse. The great scene of the world is constantly open to her view; far from seeking concealment, it is every day disclosed to her more completely, and she is taught to survey it with a firm and calm gaze. Thus the vices and dangers of society are early revealed to her; as she sees them clearly, she views them without illusions, and braves them without fear; for she is full of reliance on her own strength, and her reliance seems to be shared by all who are about her.

An American girl scarcely ever displays that virginal bloom in the midst of young desires, or that innocent and ingenuous grace which usually attend the European woman in the transition from girlhood to youth. It is rarely that an American woman at any age displays childish timidity or ignorance. Like the young women of Europe, she seeks to please, but she knows precisely the cost of pleasing. If she does not abandon herself to evil, at least she knows that it exists; and she is remarkable rather for purity of manners than for chastity of mind. . . .

II, 226 It is true that the Americans rarely lavish upon women those eager attentions which are commonly paid them in Europe; but their conduct to women always implies that they suppose them to be virtuous and refined; and such is the respect entertained for the moral freedom of the sex, that in the presence of a woman the most guarded language is used, lest her ear should be offended by an expression. In America a young unmarried woman may, alone and without fear, undertake a long journey. . . .

II, 227 As for myself, I do not hesitate to avow that, although the women of the United States are confined within the narrow circle of domestic life, and their situation is in some respects one of extreme dependence, I have nowhere seen woman occupying a loftier position; and if I were asked, now that I am drawing to the close of this work, in which I have spoken of so many important things done by the Americans, to what the singular prosperity and growing strength of that people ought mainly to be attributed, I should reply – to the superiority of their women. . . .

[Some Reflections on American Manners]

II, 230 Manners are, generally, the product of the very basis of the character of a people, but they are also sometimes the result of an arbitrary convention between certain men; thus they are at once natural and acquired.

When certain men perceive that they are the foremost persons in society, without contest and without effort – when they are constantly engaged on large objects, leaving the more minute details to others – and when they live in the enjoyment of wealth which they did not amass and which they do not fear to lose, it may be supposed that they feel a kind of haughty disdain of the petty interests and practical cares of life, and that their thoughts assume a natural greatness, which their language and their manners denote. In democratic countries manners are generally devoid of dignity, because private life is there extremely petty in its character; and they are frequently low, because the mind has few opportunities of rising above the engrossing cares of domestic interests.

True dignity in manners consists in always taking one's proper station, neither too high nor too low; and this is as much within the reach of a peasant as of a prince. In democracies all stations appear doubtful; hence it is that the manners of democracies, though often full of arrogance, are commonly wanting in dignity, and, moreover, they are never either well disciplined or accomplished. . . .

II, 232 Nothing is more prejudicial to democracy than its outward forms of behaviour: many men would willingly endure its vices, who cannot support its manners. I cannot, however, admit that there is nothing commendable in the manners of a democratic people.

Among aristocratic nations, all who live within reach of the first class in society commonly strain to be like it, which gives rise to ridiculous and insipid imitations. As a democratic people does not possess any models of high breeding, at least it escapes the daily necessity of seeing wretched copies of them. In democracies manners are never so refined as among aristocratic nations, but, on the other hand, they are never so coarse. Neither the coarse oaths of the populace, nor the elegant and choice expressions of the nobility, are to be heard there: the manners of such a people are often vulgar, but they are neither brutal nor mean. . . .

In aristocracies the rules of propriety impose the same demeanour on everyone; they make all the members of the same class appear alike, in spite of their private inclinations; they adorn and they conceal the natural man. Among a democratic people manners are neither so tutored nor so uniform, but they are frequently more sincere. They form, as it were, a light and loosely-woven veil, through which the real feelings and private opinions of each individual are easily discernible. The form and the substance of human actions, often, therefore, stand in closer relation; and if the great picture of human life be less embellished, it is more true. Thus it may be said, in one sense, that the effect of democracy is not exactly to give men any particular manners, but to prevent them from having manners at all.

The feelings, the passions, the virtues, and the vices of an aristocracy may sometimes re-appear in a democracy, but not its manners; they are lost, and vanish forever, as soon as the democratic revolution is completed. It would seem that nothing is more lasting than the manners of an aristocratic class, for they are preserved / by that class II, 233 for some time after it has lost its wealth and its power — nor so fleeting, for no sooner have they disappeared than not a trace of them is to be found; and it is scarcely possible to say what they have been as soon as they have ceased to be. A change in the state of society works this miracle, and a few generations suffice to consummate it.

The principal characteristics of aristocracy are handed down by history after an aristocracy is destroyed, but the light and exquisite touches of manners are effaced from men's memories almost immediately after its fall. Men can no longer conceive what these manners were when they have ceased to witness them; they are gone, and their departure was unseen, unfelt; for in order to feel that refined enjoyment which is derived from choice and distinguished manners, habit and education must have prepared the heart, and the taste for them is lost almost as easily as the practice of them. Thus, not only a democratic people cannot have aristocratic manners, but they neither comprehend nor desire them; and as they never have thought of them, it is to their minds as if such things had never been. Too much importance should not be attached to this loss, but it may well be regretted.

I am aware that it has not infrequently happened that the same men have had very high-bred manners and very low-born feelings: the interior of courts has sufficiently shown what imposing externals may conceal the meanest hearts. But though the manners of aristocracy do not constitute virtue, they sometimes embellish virtue itself. It was no ordinary sight to see a numerous and powerful class of men, whose every outward action seemed constantly to be dictated by a natural elevation of thought and feeling, by delicacy and regularity of taste, and by urbanity of manners. Those manners threw a pleasing illusory charm over human nature; and though the picture was often a false one, it could not be viewed without a noble satisfaction. . . .

II, 234 An American, instead of going in a leisure hour to dance merrily at some place of public resort, as the fellows of his calling continue to do throughout the greater part of Europe, shuts himself up at home to drink. He thus enjoys two pleasures; he can go on thinking of his business, and he can get drunk decently by his own fireside.

I thought that the English constituted the most serious nation on the face of the earth, but I have since seen the Americans and have changed my opinion. I do not mean to say that temperament has not a great deal to do with the character of the inhabitants of the United States, but I think that their political institutions are a still more influential cause.

I believe the seriousness of the Americans arises partly from their pride. In democratic countries even poor men entertain a lofty notion of their personal importance: they look upon themselves with complacency, and are apt to suppose that others are looking at them too. With this disposition, they watch their language and their actions with care, and do not lay themselves open so as to betray their deficiencies; to preserve their dignity, they think it necessary to retain their gravity.

Harriet Martineau

From *Retrospect of Western Travel* by Harriet Martineau. Two volumes. London (Saunders and Otley), 1838.

Harriet Martineau was a precocious child who, it is said, read *Paradise Lost* at eight, almost committing it to memory. Before she was sixteen the deafness developed that handicapped her for the rest of her life. Poverty dogged her until a series of stories popularizing various aspects of political economy brought her sudden recognition and financial security. In 1834 she went to the United States to recoup her health. For more than two years she toured the country and her name and connections were such that she had ready access to the highest levels of American society. Two books resulted from this trip: *Society in America* (1836) and *A Retrospect of Western Travel* (1838). The latter was the less pretentious and the more popular of the two and from it the selections below are taken. Harriet Martineau was an honest and diligent observer of Jackson's America and she recorded what she saw clearly and with comparative impartiality. Americans found in both her books a more balanced treatment of their society than Mrs. Trollope presented. Miss Martineau continued in a writing career, turning to novels. She completed her autobiography in 1855 in anticipation of imminent death from heart disease, but she lived on for more than two decades.

First Impressions

I, 35 THE MOMENT of first landing in a foreign city is commonly spoken of as a perfect realization of forlornness. My entrance upon American life was anything but this. The spirits of my companions and myself were in a holyday dance while we were receiving our first impressions; and New York always afterward bore an air of gayety to me from the association of the early pleasures of foreign travel.

Apartments had been secured for us at a boarding-house in Broadway, and a hackney-coach was in waiting at the wharf. The moonlight was flickering through the trees of the Battery, the insects were buzzing all I, 36 about us, the catydids / were grinding, and all sounds, except human voices were quite unlike all we had heard for six weeks. One of my companions took the sound of the catydid for a noise in her head for many hours after coming into their neighbourhood. As we rattled over the stones, I was surprised to find that the street we were in was Broadway; the lower and narrower end, however; but nothing that I saw, after all I had heard, and the panorama of New York that I had visited in London, disappointed me so much as Broadway. Its length is remarkable, but neither its width nor the style of its houses. The trees with which it is lined gave it, this first evening, a foreign air. . . .

I, 37 In our rooms we found beds with four posts, looking as if meant to hang gowns and bonnets upon; for there was no tester. The washstand was without tumbler, glass, soap, or brush-tray. The candlestick had no snuffers. There was, however, the luxury, sufficient for the occasion, that every article of furniture stood still in its place, and that the apartment itself did not rock up and down. The first few days after a voyage go far towards making one believe that some things have a quality of stability, however one may be metaphysically convinced that the sea affords a far truer hint of the incessant flux and change which are the law of the universe. If I had rejoiced in the emblem at sea, I now enjoyed the deception on land.

At five in the morning I threw up my

sash to see what I could see. I cannot conceive what travellers mean by saying that there is little that is foreign in the aspect of New York. I beheld nothing at this moment that I could have seen at home, except the sky and the grass of the courtyard. The houses were all neatly and brightly painted, had green outside blinds to every window, and an apparatus for drying linen on the roof. A young lady in black silk, with her hair neatly dressed, was mopping the steps of one house and a similar young lady was dusting the parlour of another. A large locust-tree grew in the middle of the courtyard of the house I was in, and under it was a truly American woodpile. Two negroes were at the pump, and a third was carrying muskmelons.

When the breakfast-bell rang the long and cross tables in the eating-room were filled in five minutes. The cross table, at which our hostess presided, was occupied by General Mason's family,[1] a party of Spaniards, and ourselves. The long one was filled up with families returning southward from the springs; married persons without children, who preferred boarding to housekeeping; and single gentlemen, chiefly merchants. I found this mode of living rather formidable the first day; and not all the good manners that I saw at public tables ever reconciled me to it.

From a trunk belonging to a lady of our party having been / put on board a wrong ship, we had some immediate shopping to do, and to find a mantuamaker.[2] We suspected we should soon be detained at home by callers, and therefore determined to transact our business at once, though our luggage had not arrived from the customhouse, and we were not "dressed for Broadway," as the phrase is.

In the streets I was in danger of being run down by the fire-engines, so busy were my eyes with the novelties about me. These fire-engines run along the sidepavement, stopping for nobody; and I scarcely ever walked out in New York without seeing one or more out on business, or for an airing. The novelties which amused me were the spruce appearance of all the people; the pervading neatness and brightness, and the business-like air of the children. The carmen were all well dressed, and even two poor boys who were selling matches had clean shirt-collars and whole coats, though they were barefooted. The stocks of goods seemed large and handsome, and we were less struck with the indifference of manner commonly ascribed to American storekeepers than frequently afterward. The most unpleasant circumstance was the appearance and manner of the ladies whom we saw in the streets and stores. It was now the end of a very hot summer, and every lady we met looked as if she were emerging from the yellow fever; and the languid and unsteady step betokened the reverse of health.

The heat was somewhat oppressive. We were in the warm dresses we had put on while yet at sea, as our trunks had not made their appearance. Trains of callers came in the afternoon and evening; members of Congress, candidates for state offices, fellow-passengers and their friends, and other friends of our friends; and still we were not "dressed for Broadway." In the evening the luggage of my companions was brought up, but not mine. Special orders had been issued from the custom-house that my baggage should pass without examination; and it was therefore at this moment on board ship. To-night it was too late; next morning it was Sunday, and everything in the hold was under lock and key, and unattainable till Monday. There seemed no hope of my getting out all day, and I was really vexed. I wanted to see the churches, and hear the preaching, and be doing what others were doing; but the heat was plainly too great to be encountered in any gown but a muslin one. A lady boarding in the house happened to hear of the case, / and sent her servant to say that she believed her

[1] This was General Mason, father of the governor of Michigan, and, according to Miss Martineau, the most eminent citizen of Detroit.

[2] The mantua was a kind of loose gown worn by women in Miss Martineau's day.

dresses would fit me, and that she should be happy to supply me with a gown and bonnet till my trunks should arrive. I accepted her kind offer without any scruple, feeling that a service like this was just what I should wish to render to any lady under the same circumstances; so I went to church equipped in a morning-gown and second-best bonnet of this neighborly lady's. . . .

I, 41 I was assured at the outset that the late abolition riots in New York were the work of the Irish emigrants, who feared the increase of a free black population as likely to interfere with their monopoly of certain kinds of labour. This I afterward found to be untrue. Some Irish may have joined in "the row," but the mischief originated with natives. It is remarkable that I heard no more of abolition for many weeks; I think not till I was about leaving Philadelphia. . . .

I, 42 One of the first impressions of a foreigner in New York is of the extreme insolence and vulgarity of certain young Englishmen, who thus make themselves very conspicuous. Well-mannered Englishmen are scarcely distinguishable from the natives, and thus escape observation; while every commercial traveller who sneers at republicanism all day long, and every impertinent boy, leaving home for the first time, with no understanding or sympathy for anything but what he has been accustomed to see at home, obtrudes himself upon the notice, and challenges the congeniality of such countrymen and countrywomen as he can contrive to put himself in the way of. I was annoyed this evening, on my return home, by a very complete specimen of the last-mentioned order of travellers.

Need I say, after thus detailing the little incidents which followed my landing in America, that my first impressions of the country were highly agreeable?

High Road Travelling

I, 71 Our first land travelling, in which we had to take our chance with the world in general, was across the State of New York. My account of what we saw may seem excessively minute in some of its details; but this style of particularity is not adopted without reasons. While writing my journal, I always endeavoured to bear in mind the rapidity with which civilization advances in America, and the desirableness of recording things precisely in their present state, in order to have materials for comparison some few years hence, when travelling may probably be as unlike what it is now, as a journey from London to Liverpool by the new railroad differs from the same enterprise as undertaken a century and a half ago. . . .

I, 72 In [the wayside] inns the disagreeable practice of rocking in the chair is seen in its excess. In the inn parlour are three or four rocking-chairs, in which sit ladies who are vibrating in different directions, and at various velocities, so as to try the head of a stranger almost as severely as the tobacco-chewer his stomach. How this lazy and ungraceful indulgence ever became general, I cannot imagine; but the nation seems so wedded to it, that I see little chance of its being forsaken. When American ladies come to live in Europe, they sometimes send home for a rocking-chair. A common wedding-present is a rocking-chair. A beloved pastor has every room in his house furnished with a rocking-chair by his grateful and devoted people. It is well that the gentlemen can be satisfied to sit still, or the world might be treated with the spectacle of the sublime American Senate in a new position; its fifty-two senators see-sawing in full deliberation, like the wise birds of a rookery in a breeze. If such a thing should ever happen, it will be time for them to leave off laughing at the Shaker worship. . . .

I, 83 Just after dark we arrived at Syracuse, in time for the common supper. I was surprised at the size and style of the hotel. Land and building material being cheap, and there being no window-tax, there is little inducement to economize space in the American houses, and the new hotels have the ambitious air which is given by spaciousness. The deficiency lies in furniture, and yet more in attendance; but I really think, that if travellers will trouble themselves to learn a little of the ways of the house, so as not to run into opposition to other people's convenience, much more comfort may be enjoyed in these places than unaccommodating tourists will believe. Our chambers were quite sufficiently furnished here; and I never in any place found difficulty in obtaining as large a supply of water as I wished by simply asking for it in good time. I observed that the hotel parlours in various parts of the country were papered with the old-fashioned papers, I believe French, which represent a sort of panorama of a hunting-party, a fleet, or some such diversified scene. I saw many such a hunting-party, the ladies in scarlet riding-habits, as I remember the landlord of the inn at Bray, near Dublin, to have been proud of in his best parlour. At Schenectady, the bay of Naples, with its fishing-boats on the water and groups of lazzaroni[1] on the shore, / adorned our parlour walls. It seems to be an irresistible temptation to idle visitors, English, Irish, and American, to put speeches into the mouths of the painted personages; and such hangings are usually seen deformed with scribblings. The effect is odd, in wild places, of seeing American witticisms put into the mouths of Neapolitan fishermen, ancient English ladies of quality, or of tritons and dryads.

I, 84

There is taste quite as bad as this in a matter of far more importance, the naming of places. Syracuse in the State of New York! I often wonder whether it is yet too late to revert to the Indian names, to undo the mischief which has been done by boys fresh from their smattering of the classics, who have gone into the forest to hew out towns and villages. I heard many Americans say that the State of New-York ought to be called Ontario, and the city Manhattan. But, so far from bringing back the nomenclature to a better state, we not only find Utica, Syracuse, Manlius, and Camillus, and the village of Geneva on Senaca Lake, with Ithaca at its other extremity, but the village of Chittenango actually baptized into Sullivan; and all this in the neighbourhood of the lakes Onondago, Cayuga, and Owasco. It is as bad as the English in Van Diemen's Land, who, if I remember rightly, have got Palmyra, Richmond, and Jericho all in a line. . . .

[1] In Naples, idlers who have no homes and live by odd jobs and begging. Named from the Hospital of St. Lazarus, their place of refuge.

We reached Batavia [by stage] to breakfast, and soon after found ourselves on the first piece of corduroy road we had encountered in the country. I mention this because corduroy roads appear to have made a deep impression on the imaginations of the English, who seem to suppose that American roads are all corduroy. I can assure them that there is a / large variety in American roads. There are the excellent limestone roads which stretch out in three directions from Nashville, Tennessee, and some like them in Kentucky, on which the tourist might sketch almost without difficulty while travelling at a rapid rate. There is quite another sort of limestone road in Virginia, in traversing which the stage is dragged up from shelf to shelf, some of the shelves sloping so as to throw the passengers on one another, on either side alternately. Then there are the rich mud roads of Ohio, through whose deep red sloughs the stage goes slowly sousing after rain, and gently upsetting when the rut on the one or the other side proves to be of a greater depth than was anticipated. Then there are the sandy roads of the pine-barrens, of an agreeable consistency after rain, but very heavy in dry weather. Then there is the ridge road, running parallel with a part of Lake Ontario, and supposed to be the edge of what was once its basin. The level terrace thus provided by Nature offered the foundation of an admirable road, one of the best in the states. Lastly, there is the corduroy road, happily of rare occurrence, where, if the driver is merciful to his passengers, he drives them so as to give them the asso-

I, 88

I, 89

ciation of being on the way to a funeral, their involuntary sobs on each jolt helping the resemblance; or, if he be in a hurry, he shakes them like pills in a pillbox. But the American drivers are a class of men marked by that merciful temper which naturally accompanies genius. They are men who command admiration equally by their perfection in their art, their fertility of resource, and their patience with their passengers. I was never upset in a stage but once during all my travels; and the worse the roads were, the more I was amused at the variety of devices by which we got on, through difficulties which appeared insurmountable, and the more I was edified at the gentleness with which our drivers treated female fears and fretfulness. . . .

First Sight of Slavery

I, 139 From the day of my entering the States till that of my leaving Philadelphia I had seen society basking in one bright sunshine of good-will. The sweet temper and kindly manners of the Americans are so striking to foreigners, that it is some time before the dazzled stranger perceives that, genuine as is all this good, evils as black as night exist along with it. I had been received with such hearty hospitality everywhere, and had lived among friends so conscientious in their regard for human rights, that, though I had heard of abolition riots, and had observed somewhat of the degradation of the blacks, my mind had not yet been really troubled about the enmity of the races. The time of awakening must come. It began just before I left Philadelphia.

I was calling on a lady whom I had heard speak with strong horror of the abolitionists (with whom I had then no acquaintance), and she turned round upon me with the question whether I would not prevent, if I could, the marriage of a white person with a person of colour. I saw at once the beginning of endless troubles in this inquiry, and was very sorry it had been made; but my determination had been adopted long before, never to evade the great question of colour; never to provoke it; but always to meet it plainly in whatever form it should be presented. I replied that I would never, I, 140 under any circumstances, try to / separate persons who really loved, believing such to be truly those whom God had joined; but I observed that the case she put was one not likely to happen, as I believed the blacks were no more disposed to marry the whites than the whites to marry the blacks. "You are an amalgamationist!" cried she. I told her that the party term was new to me; but that she must give what name she pleased to the principle I had declared in answer to her question. This lady is an eminent religionist, and denunciations spread rapidly from her. The day before I left Philadelphia my old shipmate, the Prussian physician, arrived there, and lost no time in calling to tell me, with much agitation, that I must not go a step farther south; that he had heard on all hands, within two hours of his arrival, that I was an amalgamationist, and that my having published a story against slavery would be fatal to me in the slave states. I did not give much credit to the latter part of this news, and saw plainly that all I had to do was to go straight on. I really desired to see the working of the slave system, and was glad that my having published against its principles divested me altogether of the character of a spy, and gave me an unquestioned liberty to publish the results of what I might observe. In order to see things as they were, it was necessary that people's minds should not be prepossessed by my friends as to my opinions and conduct; and I therefore forbade my Philadelphia friends to publish in the newspapers, as they wished, an antidote to the charges already current against me.

The next day I first set foot in a slave state, arriving in the evening at Baltimore. I dreaded inexpressibly the first sight of a slave, and could not help speculating on the lot of every person of colour I saw from the windows the first few days. The servants in the house where I was were free blacks.

Before a week was over I perceived that all that is said in England of the hatred of the whites to the blacks in America is short of the truth. The slanders that I heard of the free blacks were too gross to injure my estimation of any but those who spoke them. In Baltimore the bodies of coloured people exclusively are taken for dissection, "because the whites do not like it, and the coloured people cannot resist." It is wonderful that the bodily structure can be (with the exception of the colouring of the skin) thus assumed / to be the pattern of that of the whites; that the exquisite nervous system, the instrument of moral as well as physical pleasures and pains, can be nicely investigated on the ground of its being analogous with that of the whites; that not only the mechanism, but the sensibilities of the degraded race should be argued from to those of the exalted order, and that men come from such a study with contempt for these brethren in their countenances, hatred in their hearts, and insult on their tongues. These students are the men who cannot say that the coloured people have not nerves that quiver under moral injury, nor a brain that is on fire with insult, nor pulses that throb under oppression. These are the men who should stay the hand of the rash and ignorant possessors of power, who crush the being of creatures, like themselves, "fearfully and wonderfully made." But to speak the right word, to hold out the helping hand, these searchers into man have not light nor strength.

I, 141

It was in Baltimore that I heard Miss Edgeworth denounced as a woman of no intelligence or delicacy, whose works could never be cared for again, because, in Belinda, poor Juba was married, at length, to an English farmer's daughter![1] The incident is so subordinate that I had entirely forgotten it; but a clergyman's lady threw the volume to the opposite corner of the floor when she came to that page. As I have said elsewhere, Miss Edgeworth is worshipped throughout the United States; but it is in spite of this terrible passage, this clause of a sentence in Belinda, which nobody in America can tolerate, while no one elsewhere ever, I should think, dreamed of finding fault with it.

A lady from New-England, staying in Baltimore, was one day talking over slavery with me, her detestation of it being great, when I told her I dreaded seeing a slave. "You have seen one," said she. "You were waited on by a slave yesterday evening." She told me of a gentleman who let out and lent out his slaves to wait at gentlemen's houses, and that the tall handsome mulatto who handed the tea at a party the evening before was one of these. I was glad it was over for once; but I never lost the painful feeling caused to a stranger by intercourse with slaves. No familiarity with them, no mirth and contentment on their part, ever soothed the miserable restlessness caused by the presence of a deeply-injured fellow-being. No wonder or / ridicule on the spot avails anything to the stranger. He suffers, and must suffer from this, deeply and long, as surely as he is human and hates oppression.

I, 142

The next slave that I saw, knowing that it was a slave, was at Washington, where a little negro child took hold of my gown in the passage of our boarding-house, and entered our drawing-room with me. She shut the door softly, as asking leave to stay. I took up a newspaper. She sat at my feet, and began amusing herself with my shoestrings. Finding herself not discouraged, she presently begged play by peeping at me above and on each side of the newspaper. She was a brighteyed, merry-hearted child; confiding, like other children, and dreading no evil, but doomed, hopelessly doomed, to ignorance, privation, and moral degradation. When I looked at her, and thought of the fearful disobedience to the first of

[1] Maria Edgeworth (1767–1849) was a popular English novelist and writer of children's books. The literary quality of her novels is marred by her perpetual moral lectures.

moral laws, the cowardly treachery, the cruel abuse of power involved in thus dooming to blight a being so helpless, so confiding, and so full of promise, a horror came over me which sickened my very soul. To see slaves is not to be reconciled to slavery.

At Baltimore and Washington again I was warned, in various stealthy ways, of perils awaiting me in the South. I had no means of ascertaining the justness of these warnings but by going on, and turning back for such vague reasons was not to be thought of. So I determined to say no word to my companions (who were in no danger), but to see the truth for myself. The threats proved idle, as I suspected they would. Throughout the South I met with very candid and kind treatment. I mention these warnings partly because they are a fact connected with the state of the country, and partly because it will afterward appear that the stranger's real danger lies in the North and West, over which the South had, in my case, greatly the advantage in liberality.

Life at Washington

I, 143 Washington is no place for persons of domestic tastes. Persons who love dissipation, persons who love to watch the game of politics, and those who make a study of strong minds under strong excitements, like a season at Washington; but it is dreary to those whose pursuits and affections are domestic. I spent five weeks there, and was heartily glad when they were over. I felt the satisfaction all the time of doing something that was highly useful; of getting knowledge that was necessary to me, and could not be otherwise obtained; but the quiet delights of my Philadelphia home (though there half our time was spent in visiting) had spoiled me for such a life as every one leads at the metropolis. I have always looked back upon the five weeks at Washington as one of the most profitable, but by far the least agreeable, of my residences in the United States.

Yet we were remarkably fortunate in our domestic arrangements there. We joined a party of highly esteemed and kind friends: a member of the House of Representatives from Massachusetts, his wife and sister-in-law, and a senator from Maine. We (the above party) had a drawing-room to ourselves and a separate table at Mrs. Peyton's boarding-house; so that we formed a quiet family group enough, if only we had had any quiet in which to enjoy the privilege.

We arrived at Washington on the 13th of January, 1835, the year of the short session of Congress which closes on the 4th of March, so that we continued to see the proceedings of Congress at its busiest and most interesting time.

The approach to the city is striking to all strangers from its oddness. I saw the dome of the Capitol from a considerable distance at the end of a straight road; but, though I was prepared by the descriptions of preceding travellers, I was taken by surprise on finding myself beneath the splendid building, so sordid are the enclosures and houses on its / very verge. We went round I, 144 its base, and entered Pennsylvania Avenue, the only one of the grand avenues intended to centre in the Capitol, and a mile in a straight line from the White House, the residences of the heads of departments and the British legation.

In Philadelphia I had found perpetual difficulty in remembering that I was in a foreign country. The pronunciation of a few words by our host and hostess, the dinner-table, and the inquiries of visitors were almost all that occurred to remind me that I was not in a brother's house. At Washington it was very different. The city itself is unlike any other that ever was seen, straggling out hither and thither, with a small house or two a quarter of a mile from any other; so that, in making calls "in the city," we had to cross ditches and stiles, and walk alternately on grass and pavements, and strike across a field to reach a street.

Then the weather was so strange; sometimes so cold that the only way I could get any comfort was by stretching on the sofa drawn before the fire up to the very fender (on which days every person who went in and out of the house was sure to leave the front door wide open); then the next morning, perhaps, if we went out muffled in furs, we had to turn back and exchange our wraps for a light shawl. Then we were waited upon by a slave appointed for the exclusive service of our party during our stay. Then there were canvass-back ducks, and all manner of other ducks on the table, in greater profusion than any single article of food, except turkeys, that I ever saw. Then there was the society, singularly compounded from the largest variety of elements: foreign ambassadors, the American government, members of Congress, from Clay and Webster down to Davy Crockett, Benton from Missouri, and Cuthbert, with the freshest Irish brogue, from Georgia; flippant young belles, "pious" wives dutifully attending their husbands, and groaning over the frivolities of the place; grave judges, saucy travellers, pert newspaper reporters, melancholy Indian chiefs, and timid New England ladies, trembling on the verge of the vortex; all this was wholly unlike anything that is to be seen in any other city in the world; for all these are mixed up together in daily intercourse, like the higher circle of a little village, / and there is nothing else. You have this or nothing; you pass your days among these people, or you spend them alone. It is in Washington that varieties of manners are conspicuous. There the Southerners appear to the most advantage, and the New Englanders to the least; the ease and frank courtesy of the gentry of the South (with an occasional touch of arrogance, however) contrasting favourably with the cautious, somewhat *gauche,* and too deferential air of the members from the North. One fancies one can tell a New England member in the open air by his deprecatory walk. He seems to bear in mind perpetually that he cannot fight a duel, while other people can. The odd mortals that wander in from the western border cannot be described as a class, for no one is like anybody else. One has a neck like a crane, making an interval of inches between stock and chin. Another wears no cravat, apparently because there is no room for one. A third has his lank black hair parted accurately down the middle, and disposed in bands in front, so that he is taken for a woman when only the head is seen in a crowd. A fourth puts an arm round the neck of a neighbour on either side as he stands, seeming afraid of his tall wirehung frame dropping to pieces if he tries to stand alone; a fifth makes something between a bow and a courtesy to everybody who comes near, and poses with a knowing air: all having shrewd faces, and being probably very fit for the business they come upon. . . .

I, 145

At the president's I met a very large party, among whom there was more stiffness than I saw in any other society in America. It was not the fault of the president or his family, but of the way in which the company was unavoidably brought together. With the exception of my party, the name of everybody present began with J, K, or L; that is to say, it consisted of members of Congress, who are invited alphabetically, to ensure none being left out. This principle of selection is not, perhaps, the best for the promotion of ease and sociability; and well as I liked the day, I doubt whether many others could say they enjoyed it. When we went in the president was standing in the middle of the room to receive his guests. After speaking a few words with me, he gave me into the charge of Major Donelson, his secretary, who seated me, and brought up for introduction each guest as he passed from before the president. A congressional friend of mine (whose name began with a J) stationed himself behind my chair, and gave me an account of each gentleman who was introduced to me; where he came from, what his politics were, and how, if at all, he had distinguished himself. All this was highly amusing. At dinner the president was quite

I, 153

disposed for conversation. Indeed, he did nothing but talk. His health is poor, and his diet of the sparest. We both talked freely of the governments of England and France; I, novice in American politics as I was, entirely forgetting that the great French question was pending, and that the president and the King of the French were then bandying very hard words. I was most struck and surprised with the president's complaints of the American Senate, in which there was at that time a small majority against the administration. He told me that I must not judge of the body by what I saw it then, and that after the 4th of March I should behold a Senate more worthy of the country. After the 4th of March there was, if I remember rightly, a majority of two in favour of the government. The ground of his complaint was, that the senators had sacrificed their dignity by disregarding the wishes of their constituents. The other side of the question is, that the dignity of the Senate is best consulted by its members following their own convictions, declining instructions for the term for which they are elected. It is a serious difficulty, originating in the very construction of the body, and not to be settled by dispute.

The president offered me bonbons for a child belonging to our party at home, and told me how many children (of his nephew's and his adopted son's) he had about him, with / a mildness and kindliness which contrasted well with his tone upon some public occasions. He did the honours of his house with gentleness and politeness to myself, and, as far as I saw, to every one else. About an hour after dinner he rose, and we led the way into the drawing-room, where the whole company, gentlemen as well as ladies, followed to take coffee; after which every one departed, some homeward, some to make evening calls, and others, among whom were ourselves, to a splendid ball at the other extremity of the city.

I, 154

General Jackson is extremely tall and thin, with a slight stoop, betokening more weakness than naturally belongs to his years. He has a profusion of stiff gray hair, which gives to his appearance whatever there is of formidable in it. His countenance bears commonly an expression of melancholy gravity; though, when roused, the fire of passion flashes from his eyes, and his whole person looks then formidable enough. His mode of speech is slow and quiet, and his phraseology sufficiently betokens that his time has not been passed among books. When I was at Washington albums were the fashion and the plague of the day. I scarcely ever came home but I found an album on my table or requests for autographs; but some ladies went much further than petitioning a foreigner who might be supposed to have leisure. I have actually seen them stand at the door of the Senate Chamber, and send the doorkeeper with an album, and a request to write in it, to Mr. Webster and other eminent members. I have seen them do worse; stand at the door of the Supreme Court, and send in their albums to Chief-Justice Marshall while he was on the bench hearing pleadings. The poor president was terribly persecuted; and to him it was a real nuisance, as he had no poetical resource but Watts's hymns. I have seen verses and stanzas of a most ominous purport from Watts, in the president's very conspicous handwriting, standing in the midst of the crowquill compliments and translucent charades which are the staple of albums. Nothing was done to repress this atrocious impertinence of the ladies. I always declined writing more than name and date; but senators, judges, and statesmen submitted to write gallant nonsense at the request of any woman who would stoop to desire it. . . .

I, 158

Among our casual visitors at Washington was a gentleman who little thought, as he sat by our fireside, what an adventure was awaiting him among the Virginia woods. If there could have been any anticipation of it, I should have taken more notice of him than I did; as it is, I have a very slight recollection of him. He came from Maine, and intended before his return to visit the springs of Virginia, which he did the next summer. It seems that he talked in the stages rashly, and somewhat in a bragging style — in a style, at least, which he was not prepared to support by a harder testimony — about abolitionism. He declared that abolitionism was not so dangerous as people thought; that he avowed it without any fear; that he had frequently attended abolition meetings in the North, and was none the worse for it in the slave states, etc. He finished his visit at the Springs prosperously enough; but, on his return, when he and a companion were in the stage in the midst of the forest, they met at a crossroad — Judge Lynch; that is, a mob with hints of cowhide and tar and feathers. The mob stopped the stage, and asked for the gentleman by name. It was useless to deny his name, but he denied everything else. He denied his being an abolitionist; he denied his having ever attended abolition meetings, and harangued against abolitionism from the door of the stage with so much effect, that the mob allowed the steps to be put up, and the vehicle to drive off, which it did at full speed. It was not long before the mob became again persuaded that this gentleman was a fit object / of vengeance, and pur- I, 159 sued him; but he was gone as fast as horses could carry him. He did not relax his speed even when out of danger, but fled all the way into Maine. It was not on the shrinking at the moment that one would animadvert so much as on the previous bragging. I have seen and felt enough of what peril from popular hatred is, in this martyr age of the United States, to find it easier to venerate those who can endure than to despise those who flinch from the ultimate trial of their principles; but every instance of the infliction of Lynch punishment should be a lesson to the sincerest and securest to profess no more than they are ready to perform. . . .

Country Life in the South

I, 209 There was no end to the kind cautions given me against travelling through the Southern States, not only on account of my opinions on slavery, but because of the badness of the roads and the poverty of the wayside accommodations. There was so much of this, that my companion and I held a consultation one day, in our room at Washington, spreading out the map, and surveying the vast extent of country we proposed to traverse before meeting my relatives at New-Orleans. We found that neither was afraid, and afterward that there was no cause for fear, except to persons who are annoyed by irregularity and the absence of comfort. The evil prognostications went on multiplying as we advanced; but we learned to consider them as mere voices on the mountain of our enterprise, which must not deter us from accomplishing it. We had friends to visit at Charleston and Columbia, South Carolina; Augusta, Georgia; Montgomery, Alabama; and Mobile. At Richmond we were cautioned about the journey into South Carolina; at Charleston we were met with dreadful reports of travelling in Georgia; in Georgia people spoke of the horrors of Alabama, and so on; and, after all, nothing could well be easier than the whole undertaking. I do not remember a single difficulty that occurred all the way. There was much fatigue, of course. In going down from Richmond to Charleston with a party of friends we were nine days on the road, and had only three nights' rest. Throughout the journey we were obliged to accommodate ourselves to the stage hours, setting off sometimes in the evening, sometimes at midnight; or, of all uncomfortable seasons, at two or three in the morning. On a journey of many days, we had to inform ourselves of the longest time that the stage would stop at a supping or breakfasting place, so that we might manage to snatch an hour's sleep. While the meal was preparing, it was my wont to lie down and doze, in spite of hunger; if I could find a bed or sofa, it was well; if not, I could wrap myself in my cloak, and make a pillow on the floor, of my carpet-bag. I found that a sleep somewhat longer than this, when I could go to bed for two hours, was more fatiguing than refreshing. The being waked up to two, when I had lain down at midnight, was the greatest discomfort I experienced. But little sleep can be obtained in the stage from the badness of the roads. It was only when quite wearied out that I could forget myself for an hour or two amid the joltings and rollings of the vehicle. In Alabama, some of the passengers in the stage were Southern gentlemen coming from New York, in comparison with / whose fatigues ours were nothing. I think they had then travelled eleven days and nights with very short intervals of rest, and the badness of the roads at the end of a severe winter had obliged them to walk a good deal. They looked dreadfully haggard and nervous, and we heard afterward that one of them had become incessantly convulsed in the face after we had left them. It is not necessary, of course, to proceed without stopping in such a way as this; but it is necessary to be patient of fatigue to travel in the South at all.

I, 210

Yet I was very fond of these long journeys. The traveller (if he be not an abolitionist) is perfectly secure of good treatment, and fatigue and indifferent fare are the only evils which need be anticipated. The toils of society in the cities were so great to me that I generally felt my spirits rise when our packing began; and, the sorrow of parting with kind hosts once over, the prospect of a journey of many days was a very cheerful one. The novelty and the beauty of the scenery seemed inexhaustible; and the delightful American stages, open or closed all round at the will of the traveller, allow of everything being seen.

The American can conceive of nothing more dismal than a pine-barren on a rainy day; but the profound tranquillity made it beautiful to me, whose rainy days have been almost all spent in cities, amid the rumbling of hackney-coaches, the clink of pattens, the gurgle of spouts, and the flitting by of umbrellas. It is very different in the pine-barrens. The sandy soil absorbs the rain, so that there is no mud; the pines stand meekly drooping, as if waiting to be fed; the drip is noiseless; and the brooks and pools are seen bubbling clear, or quietly filling, while not a wing cleaves the air, each bird nestling in the covert of its domestic tree. When the rain ceases towards evening, the whole region undergoes a change. If a parting ray from the west pierces the woods, the stems look lilach in the moist light; the vines glitter before they shake off their last drops; the redbird startles the eye; the butterflies come abroad in clouds; the frogs grow noisy, and all nature wakens up fresh as from her siesta. The planter may be seen on his pacing white horse in a glade of the wood, or superintending the negroes who are repairing the fence of his estate. One black holds the large dibble, with which the holes for the stakes are made; others are warming their / hands at the fire which blazes on the ground; many hands to do slovenly work. While any light is left, the driver is apt to shorten his road by cutting across a knoll instead of winding round it; and then the wheels are noiseless on the turf; the branches crash as the vehicle is forced between the trees; and the wood-pigeons, frightened from their roost, flutter abroad.

I, 211

When the sun has gone down all is still within the stage; the passengers grow drowsy unless hunger keeps them awake. Each one nods upon his neighbour's shoulder, till a red light, gradually illuminating all the faces, and every moment growing brighter, rouses the dullest. Each tells somebody else that we are coming to a fire in the woods. First there are lines of little yellow flames on each side of the path; the blazing up of twigs too dry to have been made incombustible by the morning's rain. Then there is a pond of red fire on either hand, and pillars of light rising from it; tall burning stems, throwing out jets of flame on all sides, or emitting a flood of sparks when touched by the night breeze. The succeeding darkness is intense. The horses seem to feel it, for they slacken to a foot-pace, and the grazing of a wheel against a pinestem, or the zigzag motion of the vehicle, intimates that the driver's eyes have been dazzled. Presently the horses set off again, and the passengers sink once more into silence. They are next roused by the discordant horn of the driver, sending out as many distinct blasts as there are passengers, each blast more of a screech than the last, and the final flourish causing a shout of laughter in the coach; laughter animated a little, perhaps, by the prospect of supper. Right or left soon appears the loghouse, its open shutters and door giving token that a large fire is blazing within. The gentlemen hand out the ladies at the door, and then stand yawning and stretching, or draw to the fire while they can, before the ladies take possession of the best places. The hostess, who is busy cooking, points to a lamp, with which the ladies light themselves to her chamber, to put up their hair under their bonnets for the night. Little impish blacks peep and grin from behind the stove or shine in the heat of the chimney-corner. If any one of them has ever received a compliment on his dexterity, he serves with most ostentatious bustle, his eyes wide open, his row of white teeth all in sight, and his little body twisting about with every affectation of activity. An observer / may see some fun going on behind the mistress's back; a whisk of a carving-knife across a companion's throat, or a flourish of two plates like cymbals over the head.

I, 212

At last supper is ready; the broiled venison, the ham collops and eggs, and applesauce; the infusion which is called tea or coffee; and the reeking cornbread. Before the clatter of knives has ceased, the stage, with its fresh horses, is at the door; the ladies snatch a final warming while the driver finishes his protracted meal, their eyes being now at liberty to study the apartment, looking round for some other object than the old story, the six presidents who smile from the walls of almost every loghouse in America, and the great map of the United States, with a thumbmark, amounting to an erasure, on the spot of the very territory where this particular loghouse happens to be. If we wanted to consult a map in a hurry in such places as these, we never had to hunt out our present situation. There was always the worn spot to serve as the centre to our investigations. The passengers, however wearily they might have descended from the stage, are pretty sure to enter it again with a spring; warm and satisfied, with a joke on their tongues, and a good supper to sleep or muse upon.

The sleep seldom lasts long, however. You are sure to come to a creek, where nobody has ever erected a bridge, or where a freshet has carried one away, and no measures have been taken to rebuild it. With drowsy groans, the passengers rouse themselves, and get out at the driver's bidding under the cold stars or the drifting clouds. The ladies slip on their India-rubber shoes, for their first step may be into soft mud. They stand upon a bank if there be one, in order not to be run over in the dark; while the scow shows by the reflection of the light at her bow where the river is. When she touches the bank the driver calls to everybody to keep out of the way, cracks his whip, and drives his lumbering carriage down the bank and into the scow; the passengers follow; the scow is unchained, and the whole load is pushed across the stream, or pulled, if it happens to be a rope-ferry. When the expected shock tells you that you have arrived at the other side, the driver again cracks his whip, and the horses scramble. If they should refuse to mount the steep bank, and back a step upon the passengers instead, everyone would infallibly be driven into the river. A delicate coaxing is therefore employed; and I imagine the / animals must be aware what a ticklish thing any freak of theirs would be in such a situation, for I never knew them decline mounting the bank without a single back step.

I, 213

If the teambolt or other fastening of equal consequence should happen to break, there is a chance of two hours' rest or so. Something snaps; the vehicle stops; the gentlemen get out; the ladies gaze from the windows, while somebody half-dressed comes out with a lantern from any dwelling that may be in sight, and goes back again for hammer and nail, or, at worst, a piece of cord, and you proceed at a slow footpace to the nearest hotel. There the slaves, roused from the floor, where they are lying like dogs, go winking about, putting fresh logs on the smouldering fire, and lighting a lamp or two. After repeated inquiries on the part of the ladies, who feel the first minutes of their two hours slipping away without any promise of rest, a female slave at last appears, staring as if she had never seen anybody before. The ladies have already taken out nightcap, soap, and towel from their carpet-bags. They motion the woman up stairs, and follow her. They find the water-jug, if there be one, empty, of course. With infinite coaxing they get the attendant to fill it. Long after they are undressed it comes, clear or "sort o' muddy," as may be. If there are no sheets or yellow ones, the ladies spread their dressing-gowns over the bed, and use their cloaks for a covering. As soon as they have lain down, a draught begins to blow in the strangest way on the top of their heads. They examine, and find a broken window behind the bed. They wrap up their heads and lie down again. As soon as they are fairly dreaming that they are at home, and need not get up till they please, the horn startles them; they raise their heads, see a light under the door, and the black woman looks in to drawl out that they must please to make haste. It seems like a week since they lay down; but they are not rested, and turn away sick and dizzy from the flickering light.

In the morning you wonder where your fatigue is gone. As the day steals through the forest, kindling up beauty as it goes, the traveller's whole being is refreshed. The young aloes under the fallen trunks glitter with dew; the gray moss, dangling from the trees, waves in the breath of the morning. The busy little chameleons run along the fences, and the squirrel erects his brush as you pass. While the / crescent moon and the morning star glittered low down in the sky, you had longed to stay the sun beneath the horizon; but, now that he is come, fresh vigour and enjoyment seem to be shed down with his rays. I, 214

At such an hour you often come up with a family departing from the spot where they had "camped out" for the night. I never had the pleasure of camping out, but I know exactly what it must be like, for I have seen establishments of this sort in every stage of the process, from the searching out a spot blessed with a running stream, a shelter to windward, a dry soil, and plenty of fuel, to the piling the wagon with the pots, pans, and children previous to starting at dawn. There is a striking air of cheer about the family when beginning their new day; leaving behind the desolation they have made; the scorched turf, the scattered brushwood, chips, and meat-bones, and setting forth in renewed strength in the fresh morning. I owe to these people many a picture such as will never meet my eye in the galleries of art.

Our stationary rural life in the South was various and pleasant enough; all shaded with the presence of slavery, but without any other drawback. There is something in the make-shift, irregular mode of life which exists where there are slaves, that is amusing when the cause is forgotten.

The waking in the morning is accomplished by two or three black women staring at you from the bedposts. Then it is five minutes' work to get them out of the room. Perhaps, before you are half dressed, you are summoned to breakfast. You look at your watch, and listen whether it has stopped, for it seems not to be seven o'clock yet. You hasten, however, and find your hostess making the coffee. The young people drop in when the meal is half done, and then it is discovered that breakfast has been served an hour too early, because the clock has stopped, and the cook has ordered affairs according to her own conjectures.

Everybody laughs, and nothing ensues. After breakfast a farmer in homespun—blue trousers and an orange-brown coat, or all over gray—comes to speak with your host. A drunken white has shot one of his negroes, and he fears no punishment can be obtained, because there were no witnesses of the deed but blacks. A consultation is held whether the / affair shall go into court; and, before the farmer departs, he is offered cake and liqueur.

I, 215

Your hostess, meantime, has given her orders, and is now engaged in a back room, or out in the piazza behind the house, cutting out clothes for her slaves; very laborious work in warm weather. There may be a pretence of lessons among the young people, and something more than pretence if they happen to have a tutor or governess; but the probability is that their occupations are as various as their tempers. Rosa cannot be found; she is lying on the bed in her own room reading a novel; Clara is weeping for her canary, which has flown away while she was playing with it; Alfred is trying to ascertain how soon we may all go out to ride; and the little ones are lounging about the court, with their arms round the necks of blacks of their size. You sit down to the piano or to read, and one slave or another enters every half hour to ask what is o'clock. Your hostess comes in at length, and you sit down to work with her; she gratifies your curiosity about her "people," telling you how soon they burn out their shoes at the toes, and wear out their winter woollens, and tear up their summer cottons; and how impossible it is to get black women to learn to cut out clothes without waste; and how she never inquires when and where the whipping is done, as it is the overseer's business, and not hers. She has not been seated many minutes when she is called away, and returns saying how babyish these people are, that they will not take medicine unless she gives it to them; and how careless of each other, so that she has been obliged to stand by and see Diana put clean linen upon her infant, and to compel Bet to get her sick husband some breakfast.

Morning visitors next arrive. It may be the clergyman, with some new book that you want to look at; and inquiries whether your host sees any prospect of getting the requisite number of professors for the new college, or whether the present head of the institution is to continue to fill all the chairs. It may be a lank judge from some raw district, with a quid in his cheek, a swordcane in his hand, and a legal doubt in his mind which he wants your host to resolve. It may be a sensible woman, with courtesy in her countenance and decision in her air, who is accustomed really to rule her household, and to make the most of such human material and such a human lot as are pressing around and upon / her. If so, the conversation between her and your hostess becomes rapid and interesting; full of tales of perplexity and trouble, of droll anecdotes, and serious and benevolent plans. Or it may be a lady of a different cast, who is delighted at the prospect of seeing you soon again. You look perplexed, and mention that you fear you shall be unable to return this way. Oh, but you will come and live here. You plead family, friends, and occupation in England, to say nothing of England being your home. Oh, but you can bring your family and friends with you. You laughingly ask why. She draws up and replies, "for the honour and glory of living in a republic."

I, 216

Meantime Clara has dried her tears, for some one has recovered her canary, and the door of the cage is shut. The carriage and saddle-horses are scrambling on the gravel before the door, and the children run in to know if they may ride with you. Cake, fruit, and liqueurs, or perhaps tea, are brought in, and then the ladies depart. The clergyman thinks he will ride round with your party, hearing that you are going to inspect Mr. A.'s plantation. He warns you that it will not be "pleasant to see even the best plantations," and your trembling heart fully agrees.

You admire the horsemanship of your host on his white horse, and the boys on their black ponies. The carriage goes at good speed, and yet the fast *pace* of the saddle-horses enables the party to keep together. While you are looking out upon a picturesque loghouse, peeping forth from a blossomy thicket, or admiring a splendid hedge of the Cherokee rose in straggling bloom, Rosa rouses herself from a revery, and asks you to tell her all about Victoria.

"What shall I tell you?"

"What religion is she? A Unitarian, I suppose, like you."

Church of Englandism and dissent being explained, Rose resumes, in a plaintive voice, "Is she betrothed yet?"

"Not that I know of."

"Oh, I hope she is! I wish I knew! When will she be queen? When she is eighteen, won't she? Oh! I thought she was to be of age, and made queen at eighteen. How long will she be queen?"

"As long as she lives."

"As long as she lives! Why I thought—"

Rosa has no idea of rulers not being I, 217 changed every four / or eight years. Even her imagination is almost overpowered at the idea of being set above everybody else for life.

The carriage stops, and you are invited to step out, and view the ravages of a tornado a season or two ago; you see how clear a path it made for itself in the forest, and how it swept across the river, tearing down an answering gap through the tall canebrake on the opposite bank. The prostrated trees lie sunk in swamp; half hidden by flowering reeds and bright mosses, while their stumps, twice as tall as yourself, are all cropped off, whatever may be their thickness, precisely at the same height, and so wrenched and twisted as to convince you that you never before conceived of the power of the winds. The boys show you a dry path down to the river side, that you may see the fishtraps that are laid in the stream, and watch the couples of shad-fishers—dark figures amid the flashing waters—who are pursuing their occupation in the glare of noon. The girls tell you how father remembers the time when there were bears in the canebrake, and there was great trouble in getting them to come out of their thick covert to be killed. When father first came here, this side of the river was all canebrake too. Is not a canebrake very ugly? It may not have any picturesque beauty; but your eye rests upon it with satisfaction as a tropical feature in the scene.

You proceed, and point out with admiration a beautifully-situated dwelling, which you declare takes your fancy more than any you have seen. The children are amused that you should suppose any one lives there, overshadowed with trees as it is, so that its inhabitants would be devoured by moschetoes. [sic.] Your hostess tells you that it is called Mr. B.'s Folly. He spent a good deal of money and much taste upon it, but it is uninhabitable from being rather too near the river. The fever appeared so immediately and decisively that the family had to leave it in three months, and there it stands, to be called B.'s Folly.

Your host paces up to the carriage window to tell you that you are now on A.'s plantation. You are overtaking a long train of negroes going to their work from dinner. They look all over the colour of the soil they are walking on: dusky in clothing, dusky in complexion. An old man, blacker than the rest, is indicated to you as a native African; and you point out a child so light as to make you doubt whether he be a slave. A glance at the long heel settles the / matter. I, 218 You feel that it would be a relief to be assured that this was a troop of monkeys dressed up for sport, rather than that these dull, shuffling animals should be human.

There is something inexpressibly disgusting in the sight of a slave woman in the field. I do not share in the horror of the Americans at the idea of women being employed in outdoor labour. It did not particularly gratify me to see the cows always milked by men (where there were no slaves); and the hay and harvest fields would have looked brighter in my eyes if women had been there to share the wholesome and cheerful toil. But a negro woman behind the plough presents a very different object from the English mother with her children in the turnip-field, or the Scotch lassie among the reapers. In her pre-eminently ugly costume, the long, scanty, dirty woollen garment, with the shabby large bonnet at the back of her head, the perspiration streaming down her dull face, the heavy tread of the splay foot, the slovenly air with which she guides her plough, a more hideous object cannot well be conceived, unless it be the same woman at home, in the negro quarter, as the cluster of slave dwellings is called.

You are now taken to the cotton-gin, the building to your left, where you are shown how the cotton, as picked from the pods, is drawn between cylinders so as to leave the seeds behind; and how it is afterward packed, by hard pressure, into bales. The neighbouring creek is dammed up to supply the water-wheel by which this gin is worked. You afterward see the cotton-seed laid in handfuls round the stalks of the young springing corn, and used in the cotton field as manure.

Meantime you attempt to talk with the slaves. You ask how old that very aged man is, or that boy; they will give you no intelligible answer. Slaves never know, or never will tell their ages, and this is the reason why the census presents such extraordinary reports on this point, declaring a great number to be above a hundred years old. If they have a kind master, they will boast to you of how much he gave for each of them, and what sums he has refused for them. If they have a hard master, they will tell you that they would have more to eat and be less flogged, but that massa is busy, and has no time to come down and see that they have enough to eat. Your hostess is well known on this plantation, and her kind face has been recognised from a distance; I, 219 and already a negro woman has / come to her with seven or eight eggs, for which she knows she shall receive a quarter dollar. You follow her to the negro quarter, where you see a tidy woman knitting, while the little children who are left in her charge are basking in the sun, or playing all kinds of antics in the road; little shining, plump, cleareyed children, whose mirth makes you sad when you look round upon their parents, and see what these bright creatures are to come to. You enter one of the dwellings, where everything seems to be of the same dusky hue; the crib against the wall, the walls themselves, and the floor, all look one yellow. More children are crouched round the wood fire, lying almost in the embers. You see a woman pressing up against the wall like an idiot, with her shoulder turned towards you, and her apron held up to her face. You ask what is the matter with her, and are told that she is shy. You see a woman rolling herself about in a crib, with her head tied up. You ask if she is ill, and are told that she has not a good temper; that she struck at a girl she was jealous of with an axe, and the weapon being taken from her, she threw herself into the well, and was nearly drowned before she was taken out, with her head much hurt.

The overseer has, meantime, been telling your host about the fever having been more or less severe last season, and how well off he shall think himself if he has no more than so many days' illness this summer; how the vegetation has suffered from the late frosts, pointing out how many of the oranges have been cut off, but that the great magnolia in the centre of the court is safe. You are then invited to see the house, learning by the way the extent and value of the estate you are visiting, and of the "force" upon it. You admire the lofty, cool rooms, with their green blinds, and the width of the piazzas on both sides the house, built to compensate for the want of shade from trees, which cannot be allowed near the dwelling for fear of moschetoes. You visit the icehouse, and find it pretty full, the last winter having been a severe one. You learn that, for three or four seasons after this icehouse was built, there was not a spike of ice in the state, and a cargo had to be imported from Massachusetts.

When you have walked in the field as long as the heat will allow, you step into the overseer's bare dwelling, within its bare enclosure, where fowls are strutting about, I, 220 and refresh / yourself with a small tumbler of milk; a great luxury, which has been ordered for the party. The overseer's fishing-tackle and rifle are on the wall, and there is a medicine chest and a shelf of books. He is tall, sallow, and *nonchalant*, dropping nothing more about himself and his situation than that he does not know that he has had more than his share of sickness and trouble in his vocation, and so he is pretty well satisfied.

Your hostess reminds the party that they are going out to dinner, and that it is quite time to be returning to dress. So you go straight home by a shorter road, stopping no more, but looking out, now at a glorious trumpet honeysuckle dangling from a branch, now at a lofty, spreading green tree, red hot close to the ground, while a sheet of flame is spreading all about its roots, the flames looking orange and blue in the bright sunshine.

You are glad to find, on arriving at home, that you have half an hour to lie down before you dress, and are surprised, on rising, to feel how you are refreshed. You have not very far to go to dinner; only to Mr. E.'s cottage on the Sand Hills. The E.'s have just come for the summer, the distant city being their winter residence. If you find the accommodations poor, you must excuse it in consideration of their recent removal. The E.'s live in very good style in the city. The cottage is half way up a gentle ascent, with a deep, sandy road leading to the wooden steps of the front piazza, and pine forests in the rear. The entertainment today is not solely on your account; it is a parting dinner to young Mr. and Mrs. F., who are going to reside farther West. They are leaving their parents and friends, and the family estate, and are to live in a log-house until a proper dwelling can be built. Mrs. F. is rather low in spirits, but her mother means to send the old family nurse with her, so that she will have one comfort, at any rate, and will be able to trust her infant out of her sight now and then. As for Mrs. E., she informs you that she has come out to the cottage sooner than she usually does, as she is expecting her confinement. She has all her five children in her presence always; and as she cannot trust them for an hour with her "people," their noise and the heat would be intolerable in town; but here, where her room opens upon the piazza, she can have the children always in her sight or hearing with less fatigue than in the city. You ask whether such a / I, 221 charge be not too much for her. Certainly; but there is no use in complaining, for it cannot be helped. She never had a nurse that was not more plague than use. It is not only that the servants tell the children improper things, and teach them falsehood, but it is impossible to get the little boys' faces washed without seeing it done; and the infant may, as likely as not, be dropped into the fire or out of the window. Ladies must make the best of their lot, for they cannot help themselves.

The dinner is plentiful, including, of course, turkey, ham, and sweet potatoes; excellent claret, and large blocks of ice-cream. A slave makes gentle war against the flies with the enormous bunch of peacocks' feathers; and the agitation of the air is pleasant while the ladies are engaged in eating, so that they cannot use their own fans, which are hung by loops on the backs of their chairs. The afternoon is spent in the piazza, where coffee is served. There the ladies sit, whisking their feather fans, jesting with the children, and talking over the last English poem or American novel, or complaining bitterly of the dreadful incendiary publications which Mr. E. heard from Mr. H., who had heard it from Mr. M., that Judge R. had said that somebody had seen circulated among the negroes by some vile agent of the horrid abolitionists of the North.

You go in to tea, and find the table strewed with prints, and the piano open, and Mrs. F. plays and sings. The gentlemen have done discussing the French war and the currency, and are praising the conduct of the Committee of Vigilance; frankly informing you, as a stranger, of the reasons of its formation, and the modes of its operation in deterring abolitionists from coming into the neighbourhood, in arresting them on any suspicion of tampering with the negroes, and in punishing them summarily if any facts are established against them. While you are endeavouring to learn the nature of the crime and its evidence, you are summoned. There is going to be a storm, and your party must get home, if possible, before it comes on. In such a case Mrs. E. will say nothing in opposition to your leaving her so early. She would not be the means of exposing you to the storm. You hasten away, and reach home during the first explosion of thunder.

You find there a bouquet, sent to you with Miss G.'s compliments; a splendid I, 222 bunch of quince, yellow jessamine, / arbor vitae, hyacinths, cherry, and other blossoms. It is not nearly bedtime yet; and you sit on the sofa, fanning yourself, with the table-lamp dimmed by the momentary glare of blue lightning. Your hostess learns from the servants that poor Miss Clara went to bed in great grief, the cat having killed her canary in the afternoon. It has been a sad day for poor Clara, from the adventures of her bird; but she is now fast asleep.

Your host amuses you with anecdotes of South country life. He asks you how you were struck with Mrs. L., whose call you returned yesterday. You reply that she seems a cheerful, hearty personage, who makes the best of a poor lot; and you relate how pleased you were at the frankness with which she owned, pointing to the stocking she was darning, that she knew little of books nowadays, or of music, as she was making shirts and darning stockings for her sons all the year round. You were sorry to see such evidences of poverty; chairs with broken backs, and a piano with three legs, and a cracked flute; but glad that Mrs. L. seemed able to look on the bright side of things. Your host throws himself back, and laughs for three minutes; and, when he recovers, informs you that Mrs. L. is the wealthiest widow in the state. You protest that you looked upon her with respect as a meritorious widow, doing her best for a large family. Your host repeats that she is the richest widow in the state, and that she and all her family are odd about money. She has a sister in a neighbouring state, Mrs. M., who is even more bent upon economy. Last year Mrs. L. visited this sister, who lives in a country town. The sisters went out in Mrs. M.'s carriage, to make calls and do shopping. Mrs. L. observed that her sister's carriage was attended by a little mulatto girl, who let down the steps, and put them up, and mounted behind very dexterously. "The child is clever enough," said Mrs. L.; "but, sister, your carriage should have a proper footman. You should not be seen in town with a girl behind your carriage." Mrs. M. promised to consider the matter. The next day a spruce mulatto lad was in waiting, of whom Mrs. L. fully approved. When she looked in his face, however, as he was letting down the steps at the entrance of a store, she was struck by his remarkable likeness to the girl of yesterday, and observed upon it. Mrs. M. laughed, and owned she had got a suit of boy's clothes / made since I, 223 yesterday for the girl to wear during morning drives, and she thought this an excellent plan. Many such a story does your host amuse you with; observing that, though America has fewer humorists than England, they may be met with in abundance in rare settlements and retired districts, where they can indulge their fancies without much suffering from public opinion.

The storm abates. You are the oracle as to what o'clock it is; and, as you are confident that it is near eleven, the chamber lights are brought. You dismiss your dusky attendants, and throw yourself on your ample sofa for half an hour, to recall what you have seen and heard this day, and meditate on the scope and tendencies of Country Life in the Southern States.

City Life in the South

I, 224 . . . Two of us proceeded, in a light pretty hack-carriage, to the friend's house where we were expected. Nothing could be more considerate than our reception. A pile of English and American letters and newspapers awaited us, and our hostess knew that we must be fatigued; a fire was therefore immediately lighted in my chamber, and we were told that the day was our own; that our dinner would be sent up to us, and that we should not be expected in the drawing-room till we chose to join the family. I shall not soon forget the refreshment of lingering over family letters and London newspapers; of feeling that we were not liable to be called up in the dark for a fortnight at least; and of seeing my clothes laid in drawers, for the first time, I think, since I landed. A chest of drawers is seldom to be seen in the chambers, or, at least, in the guest-chambers of American houses. We were favoured in the article of closets with rows of pegs, but I believe I had the use of a chest of drawers only two or three times during my travels.

I, 225 A circumstance happened this day which, as being illustrative of manners, may be worth relating. The day before I left Richmond, Virginia, two companions and myself had employed a hack-carriage, driven by a black, for some hours; and, on dismissing it, had paid the fare, which we thought reasonable, two dollars and a half. The proprietor of the carriage and master of the driver had by some means heard who it was that had been his customer. Finding that I had left Richmond, he took the trouble to send the two dollars and a half down to Charleston, five hundred miles, with a message that it was not for the honour of Virginia that I should pay carriage hire! and the money was awaiting me on my arrival.

I had soon reason to perceive that Charleston deserves its renown for hospitality. A lecturer on phrenology sent us tickets for his course; six carriages were immediately placed at my disposal, and the servants came every morning for orders for the day. The difficulty was to use them all and equally; but, by employing one for the morning drive and another for the evening visiting, we contrived to show our friends that we were willing to avail ourselves of their kindnesses. I believe there was scarcely a morning during our stay when some pretty present did not arrive before I rose; sometimes it was a bouquet of hyacinths, which were extremely rare that year, from the lateness and severity of the frosts; sometimes it was a dish of preserve or marmalade; sometimes a feather fan, when the day promised to be hot; sometimes a piece of Indian work; sometimes of indigenous literary production. One morning I found on my window-seat a copy of the *Southern Review,* and a bouquet of hyacinths from General Hayne; and the next a basket of wafers from Mrs. P.; and the third a set of cambric handkerchiefs, inimitably marked with complimentary devices, from Mrs. W.

In the midst of all this there was no little watchfulness, among a totally different set of persons, about my proceedings with regard to the negroes. I had not been in the city twenty-four hours before we were amused with ridiculous reports of my championship on behalf of the blacks; and, long after I had left the place, reported speeches of mine were in circulation which were remarkably striking to me when I at length heard them. This circumstance shows how irritable the minds of the people are upon this topic. / I met with no difficulty, however, among my associates. I, 226 I made it a rule to allow others to introduce the subject of slavery, knowing that they would not fail to do so, and that I might learn as much from their method of approaching the topic as from anything they could say upon it. Before half an hour had passed, every man, woman, or child I might be conversing with had entered upon the question. As it was likewise a rule with me never to conceal or soften my own opinions, and never to allow myself to be irritated by what I heard (for it is too serious a subject to indulge frailties with), the best understanding existed between slaveholders and myself. We never quarrelled, while, I believe, we never failed to perceive the extent of the difference of opinion and feeling between us. I met with much more cause for admiration in their frankness than reason to complain of illiberality. The following may serve as a specimen of this part of our intercourse: —

The first time I met an eminent Southern gentleman, a defender of slavery, he said to me (within the half hour),

"I wish you would not be in such a hurry away. I wish you would stay a year in this city. I wish you would stay ten years, and then you would change your opinions."

"What opinions?"

"Your opinions on slavery."

"What do you know of my opinions on slavery?"

"Oh, we know them well enough: we have all read 'Demerara.' "

"Very well: now we shall understand each other; for I must tell you that I think about slavery exactly as I did when I wrote that story. Nothing that I have seen shows me that I have anything to qualify of what is said there. So now you know my opinions."

"Oh yes. I don't want to know anything more of your opinions. I want you to know mine."

"That is exactly what I want. When will you let me have them?"

We had engaged to dine with this gentleman the next week; it was now arranged that our party should go two hours earlier than the other guests, in order to hear this gentleman's exposition of slavery. He was well prepared, and his statement of facts and reasons was clear, ready, and entertaining. The fault was in the narrowness of his premises, for his whole argument was grounded on the supposition / that human rights consist in sufficient subsistence in return for labour. Before he began I told him that I fully understood his wish not to argue the question, and that I came to hear his statement, not to controvert it; but that I must warn him not to take my silence for assent. Upon this understanding we proceeded, with some little irritability on his part when I asked questions, but with no danger of any quarrel. I never found the slightest difficulty in establishing a similar clear understanding with every slaveholder I met. In the drawing-room of the boarding-house at Richmond, Virginia, three gentlemen, two of whom were entire strangers, attacked me in the presence of a pretty large company one afternoon. This was a direct challenge, which I did not think fit to decline, and we had it all out. They were irritable at first, but softened as they went on; and when, at the end of three hours, we had exhausted the subject, we were better friends than when we began.

I, 227

Some of the reports of my championship of the negroes arose from a circumstance which occurred the day after my arrival at Charleston. Our host proposed to take us up a church steeple, to obtain a view of the city and its environs. The key of the church was at the Guardhouse opposite, and our host said we might as well go for it ourselves, and thus get a sight of the Guardhouse. One of the city authorities showed us over it, and we stayed a few moments in a room where a lady was preferring a complaint against two negro boys for robbing a henroost. They were proved guilty, and sentenced to be flogged at the place of punishment at the other end of the city. . . .

I, 234

Charleston is the place in which to see those contrasting scenes of human life brought under the eye which moralists gather together for the purpose of impressing the imagination. The stranger has but to pass from street to street, to live from hour to hour in this city, to see in conjunction the extremes between which there is everywhere else a wide interval. The sights of one morning I should remember if every other particular of my travels were forgotten. I was driven around the city by a friend whose conversation was delightful all the way. Though I did not agree in all his / views of society, the thoughtfulness of his mind and the benevolence of his ex-

I, 235

ertions betokened a healthy state of feeling, and gave value to all he said. He had been a friend of the lamented Grimké; and he showed me the house where Grimké lived and died, and told me much of him; of the nobleness of his character, the extent of his attainments, and how, dying at fifty-four, he had lived by industry a long life.[1] My mind was full of the contemplation of the heights which human beings are destined to reach, when I was plunged into a new scene; one which it was my own conscientious choice to visit, but for which the preceding conversation had ill-prepared me. I went into the slave market, a place which the traveller ought not to avoid to spare his feelings. There was a table on which stood two auctioneers, one with a hammer, the other to exhibit "the article" and count the bids. The slaves for sale were some of them in groups below, and some in a long row behind the auctioneers. The sale of a man was just concluding when we entered the market. A woman, with two children, one at the breast, and another holding by her apron, composed the next lot. The restless, jocose zeal of the auctioneer who counted the bids was the most infernal sight I ever beheld. The woman was a mulatto; she was neatly dressed, with a clean apron and a yellow head-handkerchief. The elder child clung to her. She hung her head low, lower, and still lower on her breast, yet turning her eyes incessantly from side to side, with an intensity of expectation which showed that she had not reached the last stage of despair. I should have thought that her agony of shame and dread would have silenced the tongue of every spectator; but it was not so. A lady chose this moment to turn to me and say, with a cheerful air of complacency, "You know my theory, that one race must be subservient to the other. I do not care which; and if the blacks should ever have the upper hand, I should not mind standing on that table, and being sold with two of my children." Who could help saying within himself, "Would you were! so that that mother were released!" Who could help seeing in vision the blacks driving the whites into the field, and preaching from the pulpits of Christian churches the doctrines now given out there, that God has respect of persons; that men are to hold each other as property, instead of regarding each other as brethren; and that the right interpretation of the golden rule by the slaveholder is, / "Do unto your slaves as you would wish your master to do unto you if you were a slave!" A little boy of eight or nine years old, apparently, was next put up alone. There was no bearing the child's look of helplessness and shame. It seemed like an outrage to be among the starers from whom he shrunk, and we went away before he was disposed of. I, 236

We next entered a number of fine houses, where we were presented with flowers, and entertained with lively talk about the small affairs of gay society, which to little minds are great. To me every laugh had lost its gayety, every courtesy had lost its grace, all intercourse had lost its innocence. It was a relief to think of Grimké in his grave, escaped from the hell in which we were pent. If there be a scene which might stagger the faith of the spirit of Christianity itself; if there be an experience which might overthrow its serenity, it is the transition from the slavemarket to the abodes of the slavemasters, bright with sunshine, and gay with flowers, with courtesies, and mirth. . . .

I, 238 Our evening engagements were as strangely contrasted as those of the morning. We were at parties where we heard loud talk of justice and oppression; appeals to the eternal principles of the one, when the tariff was the subject, and expressions of the most passionate detestation of the other, which might, but for the presence of black faces in the rooms, lead a stranger to suppose that he was in the very sanctuary of human rights. We were at a young heiress's first ball, where every guest was

[1] Probably Thomas Smith Grimké, educator and reformer and brother of Sarah Moore and Angelina Grimké, anti-slavery crusaders and advocates of women's rights.

presented with a bouquet on entering; where the young ladies waltzed, and the young gentlemen gave a loose to their spirits, and all who were present had kindly greetings for the stranger. Nothing could be gayer than the external aspect of these entertainments; but it is impossible for the stranger to avoid being struck with the anxiety which shows itself through it all. I think I never was in society in any of the Southern cities without being asked what I would do if I had a legacy of slaves, or told, in vindictiveness or sorrow, that the prosperity of the North was obtained at the expense of the South. I was never in Southern society without perceiving that its characteristic is want of repose. It is restlessly gay or restlessly sorrowful. It is angry or exulting; it is hopeful or apprehensive. It is never content; never in such a state of calm satisfaction as to forget itself. This / peculiarity poisons the satisfaction of the stranger in the midst of the free and joyous hospitality to which he would otherwise surrender himself with inconsiderate delight. While everything is done that can be conceived of to make you happy, there is a weight pulling at your heartstrings, because you see that other hearts are heavy, and the nobler the heavier. While the host's little child comes to you at first sight, and holds up her mouth for a kiss, and offers to tell you a story, and pours out all her mirth and all her generosity upon you, the child's father tells you that there is a dark prospect before these young creatures, and Heaven knows what lot is in store for them. Your vigilance is kept active by continual suggestions that society is composed of two classes, which entertain a mortal dread of each other. If ever you forget this for an hour, it is recalled by the sight of a soldier at the corner of a street, of a decaying mansion or deserted estate, or of some anti-republican arrangement for social or domestic defence. You reproach yourself because you are anxious and cannot be deceived; and feel as if it were ingratitude to your entertainers not to think them the secure and happy people which, in alternation with their complaints of all the external world, they assure you they are.

I, 239

Our evenings were diversified with attendance upon phrenological lectures—which, however, soon ceases to be a variety, from the absolute sameness of all courses of lectures on that subject—with readings at home, and with a visit to a scene which I was strongly urged not to omit, the Saturday night's market held by the slaves.

I should have been sorry to miss this spectacle. The slaves enjoy the amusement and profit yielded by this market. They sit in rows, by lamplight, some with heaps of fruit and vegetables before them, or surrounded by articles of their own manufacture: boxes, bedsteads, baskets, and other handiworks, very cheap, and of good workmanship. The bananas, pines, imported apples, and oranges, which are seen in great abundance, are usually the property of the master; while the manufactured articles, made at spare hours, are nominally the slave's own. Some are allowed to make use of their leisure in preparing for the market, on condition of bringing their masters six dollars each per week, retaining whatever surplus they may gain. I could not learn the consequence of failing to bring in the six dollars / per week. They enjoy the fun and bustle of the market, and look with complacency on any white customers who will attend it. Their activity and merriment at market were pointed out to me as an assurance of their satisfaction with their condition, their conviction that their present position is the one they were made for, and in which their true happiness is to be found.

I, 240

At the very same moment I was shown the ruins of the church of St. Philip, destroyed by fire, as they frowned in the rear of the lamplight; and I was informed that the church had once before been on fire, but had been saved by the exertions of a slave, who "had his liberty given him for a reward."

"A reward!" said I. "What! when the slaves are convinced that their true happiness lies in slavery?"

The conversation had come to an awkward pass. A lady advanced to the rescue, saying that some few, too many, were haunted by a pernicious fancy, put into their heads by others, about liberty; a mere fancy, which, however, made them like the idea of freedom.

"So the benefactor of the city was rewarded by being indulged, to his own hurt, in a pernicious fancy?"

"Why . . . yes." . . .

CINCINNATI

II, 37 From the time of our leaving Richmond [on the Ohio, near Cincinnati] the boat went on at good speed. We ceased to wear round, to take in casks and deals at the beck of everybody on shore. The dinner was remarkably disagreeable: tough beef, skinny chickens, gray-looking potatoes, gigantic radishes, sour bread, and muddy water in dirty tumblers. The only eatable thing on the table was a saucerful of cranberries, and we had a bottle of claret with us. It was already certain that we should not reach Cincinnati so as to have a daylight view of it: our hopes were bounded to not being obliged to sit down to another meal on board.

The western sky faded while we were watching the *Hunter* pursuing the *Coquette,* two pretty little steamboats that were moving along under the shadow of the banks. Some time after dark we came in sight of long rows of yellow lights, with a flaring and smoking furnace here and there, which seemed to occupy a space of nearly two miles from the wharf where we at length stopped. I had little idea how beautiful this flaring region would appear in sunshine.

After waiting some time in the boat for the arrival of a hack, we proceeded up the steep pavement above the wharf to the Broadway Hotel and Boarding-house. There II, 38 we / were requested to register our names, and were then presented with the cards of some of the inhabitants who had called to inquire for us. We were well and willingly served, and I went to rest intensely thankful to be once more out of sight of slavery.

The next morning was bright, and I scarcely remember a pleasanter day during all my travels than this 16th of June. We found ourselves in a large boarding-house, managed by a singularly zealous and kindly master. His care of us was highly amusing during the whole time of our stay. His zeal may be judged of by a circumstance which happened one morning. At breakfast he appeared heated and confused, and looked as if he had a bad headache. He requested us to excuse any forgetfulness that we might observe, and mentioned that he had, by mistake, taken a dangerous dose of laudanum. We begged he would leave the table, and not trouble himself about us, and hoped he had immediately taken measures to relieve himself of the dose. He replied that he had had no time to attend to himself till a few minutes ago. We found that he had actually put off taking an emetic till he had gone to market and sent home all the provisions for the day. He had not got over the consequences of the mistake the next morning. The ladies at the breakfast-table looked somewhat vulgar; and it is undeniable that the mustard was spilled, and that the relics of the meal were left in some disorder by the gentlemen who were most in a hurry to be off to business. But every one was obliging; and I saw at that table a better thing than I saw at any other table in the United States, a lady of colour breakfasting in the midst of us! . . .

II, 44 The doctor [Dr. Drake, Miss Martineau's host] had at present a patient in Dr. Beecher's house, so we returned by the Theological Seminary. Dr. Beecher and his daughters were not at home. We met them on the road in their cart, the ladies returning from their school in the city, and we spent an evening there the next week. The seminary (Presbyterian) was then in a depressed condition, in consequence of the expulsion of most of the pupils for their refusal to avoid discussion of the slavery question. These expelled youths have since been founders and supporters of abolition societies; and the good cause has gained even more than the seminary has lost by the absurd tyranny practised against the students.

From this, the Montgomery road, there is a view of the city and surrounding country which defies description. It was of that melting beauty which dims the eyes and fills the heart — that magical combination of all elements — of hill, wood, lawn, river, with a picturesque city steeped in evening sunshine, the impression of which can never be lost / nor ever communicated. We ran up a knoll, and stood under a clump of beeches to gaze; and went down, and returned again and again, with the feeling that, if we lived upon the spot, we could never more see it look so beautiful.

II, 45

We soon entered a somewhat different scene, passing the slaughter-houses on Deer Creek, the place where more thousands of hogs in a year than I dare to specify are destined to breathe their last. Deer Creek, pretty as its name is, is little more than the channel through which their blood runs away. The division of labour is brought to as much perfection in these slaughter-houses as in the pin-manufactories of Birmingham. So I was told. Of course I did not verify the statement by attending the process. In my childhood I was permitted, by the carelessness of a nursemaid, to see the cutting up of the reeking carcass of an ox, and I can bear witness that one such sight is enough for a lifetime. But — to tell the story as it was told to me — these slaughter-houses are divided into apartments communicating with each other: one man drives into one pen or chamber the reluctant hogs, to be knocked on the head by another whose mallet is for ever going. A third sticks the throats, after which they are conveyed by some clever device to the cutting-up room, and thence to the pickling, and thence to the packing and branding, a set of agents being employed for every operation. The exportation of pickled pork from Cincinnati is enormous. Besides supplying the American navy, shiploads are sent to the West India Islands and many other parts of the world. Dr. Drake showed me the dwelling and slaughter-house of an Englishman who was his servant in 1818, who then turned pork-butcher, and was, in a few years, worth ten thousand dollars.

The teatable was set out in the garden at Dr. Drake's. We were waited upon, for the first time for many months, by a free servant. The long grass grew thick under our feet; fireflies were flitting about us, and I doubted whether I had ever heard more sense and eloquence at any Old World teatable than we were entertained with as the twilight drew on.

As we walked home through the busy streets, where there was neither the apathy of the South nor the disorder consequent on the presence of a pauper class, I felt strongly tempted to jump to some hasty conclusions about the happiness of citizenship in Cincinnati. I made a virtuous determination / to suspend every kind of judgment; but I found each day as exhilarating as the first, and, when I left the city, my impressions were much like what they were after an observation of twenty-four hours.

II, 46

The greater part of the next morning was occupied with visitors; but we found an interval to go out, under the guidance of friends, to see a few things which lay near at hand. We visited the Museum, where we found, as in all new museums whose rooms want filling up, some trumpery among much which is worthy to remain. There was a mermaid not very cleverly constructed, and some bad wax figures, posted like sentinels among the cases of geological and entomological specimens; but, on the whole, the Museum is highly creditable to the zeal of its contributors. There is, among other things, a pretty complete collection of the currency of the country, from the earliest colonial days, and some of other countries with it. I hope this will be persevered in, and that the Cincinnati merchants will make use of the opportunities afforded by their commerce of collecting specimens of every kind of currency used in the world, from the gilt and stamped leather of the Chinese and Siberians to the last of Mr. Biddle's twenty-dollar notes. There is a reasonable notion abroad that the Americans are the people who will bring the philosophy and practice of exchanges to perfection; and theirs are the museums in which should be found a full history of currency, in the shape of a complete set of specimens.

We visited Mr. Flash's bookstore, where we saw many good books, some very pretty ones, and all cheap. We heard there good accounts of the improved and improving literary taste of the place, shown in the increasing number of book societies, and the superior character of the works supplied to their orders. Mr. Flash and his partner are in favour of the protection of foreign literary property, as a matter of interest as well as principle.

II, 49 . . . All the parties I was at in Cincinnati were very amusing, from the diversity in the company, and in the manners of the natives of the East and West. The endeavour seems to be to keep up rather than to disuse distinctive observances, and this almost makes the stranger fancy that he has travelled a thousand miles between one evening and the next. The effect is entertaining enough to the foreign guest, but not very salutary to the temper of the residents, to judge by the complaints I heard about sectional exclusiveness. It appeared to me that the thing chiefly to be wished in this connexion was that the Easterners should make large concessions and allowance. It would be well for them to remember that it was they who chose the Western city, and not the city them; and that, if the elderly inhabitants are rather proud of their Western deeds, and ostentatiously attached to their Western symbols, this is a circumstance belonging to the place, and deliberately encountered, with other circumstances, by new residents; / [II, 50] and that, moreover, all that they complain of is an indulgence of the feelings of a single generation. When the elderly members of the society drop off, the children of all residents will wear the buckeye, or forget it alike. And it certainly appeared to me that the cool assumption by Easterners of the superiority of New-England over all other countries was, whether just or not, likely to be quite as offensive to the buckeyes as any buckeye exultation could be to the Yankees.

At one evening party the company sat round the drawing-room, occasionally changing places or forming groups without much formality. They were chiefly Yankees, of various accomplishments, from the learned lawyer who talked with enthusiasm about Channing, and with strong sense about everything but politics, in which his aristocratic bias drew him aside into something like nonsense, to the sentimental young widow, who instantly began talking to me of her dear Mr. ——, and who would return to the subject as often as I led away from it. Every place was remarkable for her dear Mr. —— having been better or worse there; and every event was measured by its having happened so long before or after her dear Mr. —— was buried. The conversation of the society was most about books, and society and its leaders at home and abroad. The manners of the lady of the house were, though slightly impaired by timidity, such as would grace any society of any country. The house, handsomely furnished, and adorned with some of the best of Beard's pictures, stood on a terrace beautifully surrounded with shrubbery, and commanding a fine view of the city.

At another party there was a great variety. An enormous buckeye bowl of lemonade, with a ladle of buckeye, stood on the hall table, and symbolical sprigs of the same adorned the walls. On entering the drawing-room I was presented with a splendid bouquet, sent by a lady by the hands of her brother, from a garden and conservatory which are the pride of the city. My first introduction was to the Catholic bishop, my next to a lady whom I thought then and afterward one of the cleverest women I met in the country. There was a slight touch of pedantry to be excused, and a degree of tory prejudice against the bulk of the human race which could scarcely be exceeded even in England; but there was a charming good-humour in the midst of it all, and a power both of observation and reasoning which commanded high respect. One Western II, 51 gentleman sidled about / in a sort of minuet step, unquestionably a gentleman as he was in all essential respects; and one young lady, who was, I fancy, taking her first peep at the world, kept her eyes earnestly fixed on the guests as they entered, bowing unconsciously in sympathy with every gentleman who bowed, and courtesying with every lady who courtesied. She must have been well practised in salutation before the evening was over, for the party was a large one. All the rest, with the exception of a forward Scotchman, were well-bred, and the evening passed off very pleasantly amid brisk conversation, mirth, and excellent refreshments.

Another party was at the splendid house to which the above-mentioned garden and conservatory belong. The proprietor has a passion for gardening, and his ruling taste seems likely to be a blessing to the city. He employs four gardeners, and toils in his grounds with his own hands. His garden is on a terrace which overlooks the canal, and the most parklike eminences form the background of the view. Between the garden and the hills extend his vineyards, from the produce of which he has succeeded in making twelve kinds of wine, some of which are highly praised by good judges. Mr. Longworth himself is sanguine as to the prospect of making Ohio a wine-growing region, and he has done all that an individual can to enhance the probability. In this house is West's preposterous picture of Ophelia, the sight of which amazed me after all I had heard of it. It is not easy to imagine how it should have obtained the reputation of being his best while his Cromwell is in existence. The party at this house was the largest and most elegant of any that I attended in Cincinnati. Among many other guests, we met one of the judges of the Supreme Court, a member of Congress and his lady, two Catholic priests, Judge Hall, the popular writer, with divines, physicians, lawyers, merchants, and their families. The spirit and superiority of the conversation were worthy of the people assembled.

The morning of the 19th shone brightly down on the festival of the day. It was the anniversary of the opening of the Common Schools. Some of the schools passed our windows in procession, their banners dressed with garlands, and the children gay with flowers and ribands. A lady who was sitting with me remarked, "This is our populace." I thought of the expression months afterward, when *the gentlemen* / II, 52 of Cincinnati met to pass resolutions on the subject of abolitionism, and when one of the resolutions recommended mobbing as a retribution for the discussion of the subject of slavery; the law affording no punishment for free discussion. Among those who moved and seconded these resolutions, and formed a deputation to threaten an advocate of free discussion, were some of the merchants who form the aristocracy of the place; and the secretary of the meeting was the accomplished lawyer whom I mentioned above, and who told me that the object of his life is law reform in Ohio! The "populace" of whom the lady was justly proud have, in no case that I know of, been the law-breakers; and in as far as "the populace" means not "the multitude," but the "vulgar," I do not agree with the lady that these children were the populace. Some of the patrons and prizegivers afterward proved themselves "the vulgar" of the city.

The children were neatly and tastefully dressed. A great improvement has taken place in the costume of the little boys in England within my recollection, but I never saw such graceful children as the little boys in America, at least in their summer dress. They are slight, active, and free. I remarked that several were barefoot, though in other respects well clad; and I found that many put off shoes and stockings from choice during the three hot months. Others were barefoot from poverty; children of recent settlers, and of the poorest class of the community. . . .

II, 54 Before eight o'clock in the evening the Cincinnati public was pouring into Mrs. Trollope's bazar, to the first concert ever offered to them. This bazar is the great deformity of the city. Happily, it is not very conspicuous, being squatted down among houses nearly as lofty as the summit of its dome. From my window at the boarding-house, however, it was only too distinctly visible. It is built of brick, and has Gothic windows, Grecian pillars, and a Turkish dome, and it was originally ornamented with Egyptian devices which have, however, all disappeared under the brush of the whitewasher. The concert was held in a large plain room, where a quiet, well-mannered audience was collected. There was something extremely interesting in the spectacle of the first public introduction of music into this rising city. One of the best performers was an elderly man, clothed from head to foot in gray homespun. He was absorbed in his enjoyment; so intent on his violin, that one might watch the changes of his pleased countenance the whole performance through without fear of disconcerting him. There was a young girl, in a plain white frock, with a splendid voice, a good ear, and a love of warbling which carried her through very well indeed, though her own taste had obviously been her only teacher. If I remember right, there were about five-and-twenty instrumental performers, and six or seven vocalists, besides a long row for the closing chorus. It was a most promising beginning. The thought came across me how far we were from the musical regions of the Old World, and how lately this place had been a canebrake, echoing with the bellow and growl of wild beast; and here was the spirit of Mozart swaying and inspiring a silent crowd as if they were assembled in the chapel at Salzburg!

This account of our first three days at Cincinnati will convey a sufficient idea of a stranger's impressions of the place. There is no need to give a report of its charitable institutions and its commerce; the details of the latter are well known to those whom they may concern; and in / America, II, 55 wherever men are gathered together, the helpless are aided and the suffering relieved. The most threatening evil to Cincinnati is from the faithlessness which manifests itself in illiberality. The sectional prejudice of the two leading classes of inhabitants has been mentioned, and also the ill-principled character of the opposition made to abolitionism. The offence against freedom, not only of opinion, but of action, was in this case so rank, that the citizens of Louisville, on the slaveholding side of the Ohio, taunted the citizens of Cincinnati with persecuting men for opinion from mercenary interest; with putting down free discussion from fear of injury to their commerce. A third direction in which this illiberality shows itself is towards the Catholics. The Catholic religion spreads rapidly in many or most of the recently settled parts of the United States, and its increase produces an almost insane dread among some Protestants, who fail to see that no evils that the Catholic religion can produce in the present state of society can be so afflictive and dangerous as the bigotry by which it is proposed to put it down. The removal to Cincinnati of Dr. Beecher, the ostentatious and virulent foe of the Catholics, has much quickened the spirit of alarm in that region.[1] It is to be hoped that Dr. Beecher and the people of Cincinnati will remember what has been the invariable consequence in America of public denunciations of assumed offences which the law does not reach; namely, mobbing. It is to be hoped that all parties will remember that Dr. Beecher preached in Boston three ser-

[1] Lyman Beecher (1775–1863), Presbyterian clergyman who came to Cincinnati in 1832 as pastor of the Second Presbyterian Church and head of the new seminary. Father of Henry Ward Beecher.

mons vituperative of the Catholics the Sunday before the burning of the Charlestown convent by a Boston mob. Circumstances may also have shown them by this time how any kind of faith grows under persecution; and, above all, it may be hoped that the richer classes of citizens will become more aware than they have yet proved themselves to be of their republican (to say nothing of their human) obligation to refrain from encroaching, in the smallest particulars, on their brethren's rights of opinion and liberty of conscience.

The roads in the interior of Ohio were in so bad a state from recent rains that I did not, at this time, attempt to visit the middle or northern parts of the state, where may be seen those monuments of an extinct race about which much antiquarian inquiry is going forward. One of the large mounds, whose uses are yet unexplained, and in II, 56 which are found / specimens of the arts of life which are considered to show that their artificers were not of Indian race, still remains within the city. It was crumbling away when I saw it, being a tempting spot for children's play. It is a pity it should not be carefully preserved; for the whole history of evidence, particularly the more recent portion of it, shows the impossibility of anticipating what revelations may emanate from a single object of historical interest.

A volume might presently be filled with descriptions of our drives about the environs of Cincinnati. There are innumerable points of view whence the city, with its masses of building and its spires, may be seen shining through the limpid atmosphere, like a cloud-city in the evening sky. There are many spots where it is a relief to lose the river from the view, and to be shut in among the brilliant green hills, which are more than can be numbered. But there is one drive which I almost wonder the inhabitants do not take every summer day, to the Little Miami bottoms. We continued eastward along the bank of the river for seven miles, the whole scenery of which was beautiful; but the unforgotten spot was the level about the mouth of the Little Miami river, the richest of plains or level valleys, studded with farmhouses, enlivened with clearings, and kept primitive in appearance by the masses of dark forest which filled up all the unoccupied spaces. Upon this scene we looked down from a great height, a Niphates of the New World. On entering a little pass between two grassy hills, crested with wood, we were desired to alight. I ran up the ascent to the right, and was startled at finding myself on the top of a precipice. Far beneath me ran the Little Miami, with a narrow white pebbly strand, arrow-like trees springing over from the brink of the precipice, and the long evening shadows making the current as black as night, while the green, up to the very lips of the ravine, was of the sunniest, in the last flood of western light.

For more reasons than one I should prefer Cincinnati as a residence to any other large city of the United States. Of these reasons not the last would be that the "Queen of the West" is enthroned in a region of wonderful and inexhaustible beauty. . . .

Signs of the Times in Massachusetts

II, 159 Some few years hence it will be difficult to believe what the state of the times was in some parts of the United States, and even in the maritime cities, in 1835. The system of terrorism seems now to be over. It did not answer its purpose, and is dropped; but in 1835 it was new and dreadful. One of the most hideous features of the times was the ignorance and unconcern of a large portion of society about what was being done and suffered by other divisions of its members. I suppose, while Luther was toiling and thundering, German ladies and gentlemen were supping and dancing as usual; and while the Lollards were burning, perhaps little was known or cared about it in warehouses and upon farms. So it was in America. The gentry with whom I chiefly associated in New-York knew little of the troubles of the abolitionists in that city, and nothing about the state of the anti-slavery question in their own region. In Boston I heard very striking facts which had taken place in broad daylight vehemently and honestly denied by many who happened to be ignorant of what had been done in their very streets. Not a few persons applied to me, a stranger, for information about the grand revolution of the time which was being transacted, not only on their own soil, but in the very city of their residence. A brief sketch of what I saw and experienced in Boston during the autumn of 1835 will afford some little information as to what the state of society actually was.

II, 160 At the end of August a grand meeting was held at Faneuil Hall in Boston. The hall was completely filled with the gentry of the city, and some of the leading citizens took the responsibility and conducted the proceedings of the day. The object of the meeting was to soothe the South, by directing public indignation upon the abolitionists. The pretext of the assembly was, that the Union was in danger; and though the preamble to the resolutions declared disapprobation of the institution of slavery, the resolutions themselves were all inspired by fear of or sympathy with slaveholders. They reprobated all agitation of the question, and held out assurances to the South that every consideration should be made subordinate to the grand one of preserving the Union. The speeches were a disgrace to the constituents of a democratic republic, pointed as they were against those rights of free discussion and association at the time acted upon by fellow-citizens, and imbued with deference for the South. In the crowded assembly no voice was raised in disapprobation except when a speaker pointed to the portrait of Washington as "that slaveholder;" and even then the murmur soon died into silence. The gentlemen went home, trusting that they had put down the abolitionists and conciliated the South. In how short a time did the new legislature of the State pass, in that very city, a series of thorough-going abolition resolutions, sixteen constituting the minority! while the South had already been long despising the half-and-half doctrine of the Faneuil Hall meeting!

Meantime, the immediate result of the proceeding was the mob of which I have elsewhere given an account. After that mob the regular meetings of the abolitionists were suspended for want of a place to meet in. Incessant attempts were made to hire any kind of public building, but no one would take the risk of having his property destroyed by letting it to so obnoxious a set of people. For six weeks exertions were made in vain. At last a Boston merchant, who had built a pleasant house for himself and his family, said, that while he had a roof over his head, his neighbours should not want a place in which to hold a legal meeting for honest objects; and he sent an offer of his house to the ladies of the Anti-slavery Society. They appointed their meeting for three o'clock in the afternoon of Wednesday, November 18. They / II, 161 were obliged to make known their intentions as they best could, for no newspaper would admit their advertisements, and the clergy rarely ventured to give out their notices, among others, from the pulpit.

I was at this time slightly acquainted with three or four abolitionists, and I was distrusted by most or all of the body who took any interest in me at all. My feelings were very different from theirs about the slaveholders of the South; naturally enough, as these Southern slaveholders were nothing else in the eyes of abolitionists, while to me they were, in some cases, personal friends, and, in more, hospitable entertainers. It was known, however, that I had declared my intention of attending an abolition meeting. This was no new resolution. From the outset of my inquiry into the question, I had declared that, having attended colonization meetings, and heard all that the slaveholders had to say for themselves and against abolitionists, I felt myself bound to listen to the other side of the question. I always professed my intention of seeking acquaintance with the abolitionists, though I then fully and involuntarily believed two or three charges against them which I found to be wholly groundless. The time was now come for discharging this duty.

On the Monday, two friends, then only new acquaintances, called on me at the house of a clergyman where I was staying, three miles from Boston. A late riot at Salem was talked over, a riot in which the family of Mr. Thompson had been driven from one house to another three times in one night, the children being snatched from their beds, carried abroad in the cold, and injuriously terrified. It was mentioned that the ladies of the Anti-slavery Society were going to attempt a meeting on the next Wednesday, and I was asked whether I was in earnest in saying that I would attend one of their meetings. Would I go to this one if I should be invited? I replied that it depended entirely on the nature of the meeting. If it was merely a meeting for the settlement of accounts and the despatch of business, where I should not learn what I wanted, I should wait for a less perilous time; if it was a *bona fide* public meeting, a true reflection of the spirit and circumstances of the time and the cause, I would go. The matter was presently decided by the arrival of a regular official invitation to me to attend the meeting, and to carry with II, 162 me the friend who was my / travelling companion, and any one else who might be disposed to accompany me.

Trifling as these circumstances may now appear, they were no trifles at the time; and many considerations were involved in the smallest movement a stranger made on the question. The two first things I had to take care of were to avoid involving my host in any trouble I might get into, and to afford opportunity to my companion to judge for herself what she would do. My host had been reviled in the newspapers already for having read a notice (among several others) of an anti-slavery meeting from Dr. Channing's pulpit, where he was accidentally preaching.[1] My object was to prevent his giving an opinion on anything that I should do, that he might not be made more or less responsible for my proceedings. I handed the invitation to my companion, with a hint not to speak of it. We separately made up our minds to go, and announced our determination to our host and hostess. Between joke and earnest, they told us we should be mobbed; and the same thing was repeated by many who were not in joke at all.

At two o'clock on the Wednesday we arrived at the house of a gentleman where we were to meet a few of the leading abolitionists, and dine, previous to the meeting. Our host was miserably ill that day, unfit to be out of his chamber; but he exerted himself to the utmost, being resolved to escort his wife to the meeting. During dinner, the conversation was all about the Southern gentry, in whose favour I said all I could, and much more than the party could readily receive; which was natural enough, considering that they and I looked at the people of the South from different points of view. Before we issued forth on our expedition I was warned once more that exertions had been made to get up a mob, and that it was possible we might be dispersed by violence. When we turned into the street where the house of meeting stood, there were about a dozen boys hooting before the door, as they saw ladies of colour entering. We were admitted without having to wait an instant on the steps, and the door was secured behind us.

The ladies assembled in two drawing-rooms, thrown into one by the folding-doors being opened. The total number was a hundred and thirty. The president sat at a small table by the folding-doors, and before her was a large Bible, paper, pens, and ink, and the secretary's papers. There / II, 163

[1] William Ellery Channing, foremost Unitarian minister of the period, friend of the slave, and staunch advocate of American cultural independence.

were only three gentlemen in the house, its inhabitant, the gentleman who escorted us, and a clergyman who had dined with us. They remained in the hall, keeping the front door fastened, and the back way clear for our retreat, if retreat should be necessary. But the number of hooters in the streets at no time exceeded thirty, and they treated us to nothing worse than a few yells.

A lady who sat next me amused me by inquiring, with kindness, whether it revolted my feelings to meet thus in assembly with people of colour. She was as much surprised as pleased with my English deficiency of all feeling on the subject. My next neighbour on the other hand was Mrs. Thompson, the wife of the anti-slavery lecturer, who had just effected his escape, and was then on the sea. The proceedings began with the reading of a few texts of Scripture by the president. My first impression was that the selection of these texts gave out a little vainglory about the endurance of persecution; but when I remembered that this was the reunion of persons who had been dispersed by a mob, and when I afterward became aware how cruelly many of the members had been wounded in their moral sense, their domestic affections, and their prospects in life, I was quite ready to yield my too nice criticism. A prayer then followed, the spirit of which appeared to me perfect in hopefulness, meekness, and gentleness. While the secretary was afterward reading her report, a note was handed to me, the contents of which sunk my spirits fathom deep for the hour. It was a short pencil note from one of the gentlemen in the hall; and it asked me whether I had any objection to give a word of sympathy to the meeting, fellow-labourers as we had long been in behalf of the principles in whose defence they were met. The case was clear as daylight to my conscience. If I had been a mere stranger, attending with a mere stranger's interest to the proceedings of a party of natives, I might and ought to have declined mixing myself up with their proceedings. But I had long before published against slavery and always declared my conviction that this was a question of humanity, not of country or race; a moral, not a merely political question; a general affair, and not one of city, state, party, or nation. Having thus declared on the safe side of the Atlantic, I was bound to act up to my declaration on the unsafe side, if called upon. I thought it a pity that the call had been made, though I am / now very glad that it was, as it was **II, 164** the means of teaching me more of the temper and affairs of the times than I could have known by any other means, and as it ripened the regard which subsisted between myself and the writer of the note into a substantial, profitable, and delightful friendship; but, at the moment, I foresaw none of these good consequences, but a formidable array of very unpleasant ones. I foresaw that almost every house in Boston, except those of the abolitionists, would be shut against me; that my relation to the country would be completely changed, as I should be suddenly transformed from being a guest and an observer to being considered a missionary or a spy; and results even more serious than this might reasonably be anticipated. During the few minutes I had for consideration, the wife of the writer of the note came to me, and asked what I thought of it, begging me to feel quite at liberty to attend to it or not, as I liked. I felt that I had no such liberty. I was presently introduced to the meeting, when I offered the note as my reason for breaking the silence of a stranger, and made the same declarations of my abhorrence of slavery and my agreement in the principles of the abolitionists which I had expressed throughout the whole of my travels through the South.

Of the consequences of this simple affair it is not my intention to give any account, chiefly because it would be impossible to convey to my English readers my conviction of the smallness of the portion of American society which was concerned in the treatment inflicted upon me. The hubbub was so great, and the modes of insult were so various, as to justify distant observers in concluding that the whole nation had risen against me. I soon found how few can make a great noise, while the many are careless or ignorant of what is going on about a person or a party with whom they have nothing to do; and while not a few are rendered more hearty in their regard and more generous in their hospitality by the disgraces of the individual who is under the oppression of public censure. All that I anticipated at the moment of reading the note came to pass, but only for a time. Eventually, nothing remained which in the slightest degree modified my opinions or impaired my hopes of the society I was investigating.

The secretary's report was drawn up with remarkable ability, and some animating and II, 165 beautiful letters were read / from distant members of the association. The business which had been interrupted by violence was put in train again; and, when the meeting broke up, a strong feeling of satisfaction visibly pervaded it. The right of meeting was vindicated; righteous pertinacity had conquered violence, and no immediate check to the efforts of the society was to be apprehended.

The trials of the abolitionists of Boston were, however, not yet over. Two months before, the attorney-general of the state had advocated in council the expected demand of the South, that abolitionists should be delivered up to the Slave States for trial and punishment under Southern laws. This fact is credible to those, and, perhaps, to those only, who have seen the pamphlet in reply to Dr. Channing's work on Slavery attributed to this gentleman. The South was not long in making the demand. Letters arrived from the governors of Southern States to the new governor of Massachusetts, demanding the passing of laws against abolitionism in all its forms. The governor, as was his business, laid these letters before the legislature of his state. This was the only thing he could do on this occasion. Just before, at his entrance upon his office, he had aimed his blow at the abolitionists in the following passages of his address. The same delusion (if it be mere delusion) is visible here that is shared by all persons in power, who cannot deny that an evil exists, but have not courage to remove it; a vague hope that "fate, or Providence, or something," will do the work which men are created to perform; men of principle and men of peace, like the abolitionists; victims, not perpetrators of violence. "As the genius of our institutions and the character of our people are entirely repugnant to laws impairing the liberty of speech and of the press, even for the sake of repressing its abuses, the patriotism of all classes of citizens must be invoked to abstain from a discussion which, by exasperating the master, can have no other effect than to render more oppressive the condition of the slave; and which, if not abandoned, there is great reason to fear will prove the rock on which the Union will split." . . . "A conciliatory forbearance," he proceeds to say, "would leave this whole painful subject where the Constitution leaves it, with the states where it exists, and in the hands of an all-wise Providence, who in his own good time is able to cause it to disappear, like the slavery of the ancient world, under the / gradual II, 166 operation of the gentle spirit of Christianity." The time is at hand. The "gradual operation of the gentle spirit of Christianity" had already educated the minds and hearts of the abolitionists for the work they are doing, but which the governor would fain have put off. It thus appears that they had the governor and attorney-general of the state against them, and the wealth, learning, and power of their city. It will be seen how their legislature was affected towards them.

As soon as they were aware of the demands of the Southern governors, they petitioned their legislature for a hearing, according to the invariable practice of persons who believe that they may be injured by the passing of any proposed law. The hearing was granted, as a matter of course; and a committee of five members of the legislature was appointed to hear what the abolitionists had to say. The place and time appointed were the Senate Chamber, on the afternoon of Friday, the 4th of March.

The expectation had been that few or none but the parties immediately concerned would be present at the discussion of such a "low subject;" but the event proved that more curiosity was abroad than had been supposed. I went just before the appointed hour, and took my seat with my party, in the empty gallery of the Senate Chamber. The abolitionists dropped in one by one; Garrison, May, Goodell, Follen, E. G. Loring, and others. The committee treated them with ostentatious neglect, dawdling away the time and keeping them waiting a full hour beyond the appointed time. The gallery filled rapidly, and more and more citizens entered the room below. To our great delight, Dr. Channing made his appearance there. At length it was manifest that the Senate Chamber was not large enough; and we adjourned to the Hall of Representatives, which was soon about two thirds filled.

I could not have conceived that such conduct could have been ventured upon as that of the chairman of the committee. It was so insulting as to disgust the citizens present, whatever might be their way of thinking on the question which brought them together. The chairman and another of the five were evidently predetermined. They spared no pains in showing it, twisting the meaning of expressions employed by the pleaders, noting down any disjointed phrase which could be made to tell against II, 167 those who used it, conveying / sarcasms in their questions and insult in their remarks. Two others evidenced a desire to fulfil their function, to hear what the abolitionists had to say. Dr. Channing took his seat behind the pleaders; and I saw with pleasure that he was handing them notes, acting on their side as decisively, and almost as publicly as if he had spoken. After several unanswerable defences against charges had been made, and Mr. Loring had extorted the respect of the committee by a speech in which he showed that a legislative censure is more injurious than penal laws, it was Dr. Follen's turn to speak.[2] He was presently stopped by the chairman, with a command that he should be respectful of the committee; with an intimation that the gentlemen were heard only as a matter of favour. They protested against this, their hearing having been demanded as a matter of right; they refused to proceed, and broke up the conference.

Much good was done by this afternoon's proceedings. The feeling of the bystanders was, on the whole, decidedly in favour of the pleaders, and the issue of the affair was watched with much interest. The next day the abolitionists demanded a hearing as a matter of right; and it was granted likewise as an affair of course. The second hearing was appointed for Tuesday the 8th, at the same place and hour.

Some well-meaning friends of the abolitionists had in the interval advised that the most accomplished, popular, and gentlemanly of the abolitionists should conduct the business of the second day; that the speeches should be made by Dr. Follen, Messrs. Loring and Sewall, and one or two more; and that Garrison and Goodell, the homely, primitive, and eminently suffering men of the apostleship, should be induced to remain in the background.[3] The advice was righteously rejected; and, as it happened, theirs were the speeches that went farthest in winning over the feeling of the audience to their side. I shall never forget the swimming eye and tremulous voice with which a noble lady of the persecuted party answered such a suggestion as I have mentioned. "Oh," said she, "above all things, we must be just and faithful to Garrison. You do not know what we know; that, unless we put him, on every occasion, into the midst of the *gentlemen* of the

[2] Charles Follen was a German liberal refugee who became the first professor of German literature at Harvard and was an abolitionist and Unitarian minister.

[3] William Lloyd Garrison, editor of *The Liberator*, was the dominating figure in launching the campaign against slavery; William Goodell was a reformer who helped to organize the American Anti-Slavery Society.

party, he will be torn to pieces. Nothing can save him but his being made one with those whom his enemies will not dare to touch." As for Mr. Goodell, he had been II, 168 frequently stoned. "He was / used to it." They appeared in the midst of the professional gentlemen of the association, and did the most eminent service of the day.

The hall was crowded, and shouts of applause broke forth as the pleaders demolished an accusation or successfully rebutted the insolence of the chairman. Dr. Follen was again stopped, as he was showing that mobs had been the invariable consequence of censures of abolitionism passed by public meetings in the absence of gag-laws. He was desired to hold his tongue, or to be respectful of the committee; to which he replied, in his gentlest and most musical voice, "Am I, then, to understand that, in speaking ill of mobs, I am disrespectful to the committee?" The chairman looked foolish enough during the applauses which followed this question. Dr. Follen fought his ground inch by inch, and got out all he had to say. The conduct of the chairman became at last so insufferable, that several spectators attempted a remonstrance. A merchant was silenced; a physician was listened to, his speech being seasoned with wit so irresistible as to put all parties into good-humour.

The loudly-expressed opinion of the spectators as they dispersed was, that the chairman had ruined his political career, and probably, filled the chair of a committee of the legislature for the last time. The result of the affair was that the report of the committee "spoke disrespectfully" of the exertions of the abolitionists, but rejected the suggestion of penal laws being passed to control their operations. The letters from the South therefore remained unanswered.

The abolitionists held a consultation whether they should complain to the legislature of the treatment their statements had received, and of the impediments thrown in the way of their self-justification. They decided to let the matter rest, trusting that there were witnesses enough of their case to enlighten the public mind on their position. A member of the legislature declared in his place what he had seen of the treatment of the appellants by the chairman, and proposed that the committee should be censured. As the aggrieved persons made no formal complaint, however, the matter was dropped. But the faith of the abolitionists was justified. The people were enlightened as to their position; and in the next election they returned a set of representatives, one of whose earliest acts was to pass a series of anti-slavery resolutions by a majority of 378 to 16.

These were a few of the signs of the II, 169 times in Massachusetts when I was there. They proved that, while the aristocracy of the great cities were not to be trusted to maintain the great principles on which their society was based, the body of the people were sound.

Charles Augustus Murray

From *Travels in North America* by Charles Augustus Murray. Two volumes. London (Richard Bentley), 1839.

Charles Augustus Murray's was a colorful career. Second son of the fifth earl of Dunmore he was educated at Eton and Oxford where he balanced a strong taste and marked talent for general literature and classical studies with unusual athletic prowess. On a bet he rode horseback from Oxford to London and back — a distance of 60 miles each way — in one day. While in London he took a turn in the park, dined at a gentlemen's club, saw one act of a play and managed to get back to the gate of his college at Oxford three minutes before midnight. Murray sailed for America in 1834. Among other things during three years of sightseeing in the United States he spent three months living with a group of Pawnee Indians. He saw more of frontier conditions than did many travelers of the period and although he responded sympathetically to its democracy he was repelled by the violence and brutality of the back country. His *Travels in North America,* published first in 1839, went into several editions and it is notable for its emphasis on Indians and for its author's unusually polite and gentle treatment of Americans and their society. Although he wrote other books, Murray's subsequent career was in the diplomatic service where he held responsible posts in Italy, Egypt, Switzerland, Denmark, and Portugal. After retiring from service in 1874, his remaining years were spent in cultivated leisure. He died in Paris in 1895.

[In New York]

I, 61 MY FIRST desire on landing [in New York] was to procure a glass of fresh water, a luxury so long unknown. On applying for some cool draught, a glass of excellent iced punch was put into my hands. Two goblets of this delicious beverage did I quaff, when the intense heat of the weather, and the quarantine hospital immediately opposite to me, conjured up before my eyes the spectre of cholera, and a call for the third died upon my lips.

In forty minutes we had crossed the bay, and landed at New York, near the battery; a sort of round wooden building, with an adjacent garden, which appears to answer the purpose of a kind of Marine Vauxhall. Here we hired a hack, (for so is a New York hackney coach denominated,) and drove to the American hotel, a distance of about three quarters of a mile. On arriving we inquired the coachman's charge, and I, 62 found that / here, as elsewhere, a stranger runs considerable risk of submitting to an operation which passes in England by the various names of "being done," "screwed," "taken in," "sold," "fleeced," etc. In America the appropriate phrase is "shaved;" and the fare due being three shillings, our Jehu modestly required only three dollars. After some dispute we gave him two and a half; and as he went away, one would have thought, from the expression of his face, that we had cheated him, although the fellow had received more than five shillings above his fare.

In justice to America I must subjoin two observations; first, that this class of street-plunderer is common to every city in Europe; and, secondly, that the individual in question was evidently from that "first gem of the sea," whose sons perform the greater portion of laborious and domestic service throughout the Transatlantic cities.

At five o'clock I dined for the first time at an American *table d'hote,* and I certainly never saw, at any hotel in Europe, a dinner for so large a party served in better style, or with less confusion. The dishes were very numerous, and the cookery respectable. I observed also that the knives, glasses, plates, etc. were remarkably clean, the table-cloth of the finest quality, and that ice was applied in a profusion not less unexpected than agreeable to the water, salad, cucumber, butter, etc.

In answer to my inquiries, I learnt from I, 63 one of / my neighbours that this was called the ladies' ordinary, being attended by the families resident in the house, and that the usual public *table d'hote* was daily at two o'clock, so that if I chose to attend it, I should witness a very different scene from the well-conducted table now before me. I certainly remarked that there was less conversation than at a German *table d'hote,* perhaps even less than at an English public table; and although the dinner was a ceremony quickly despatched, there was neither haste nor scrambling such as travellers are led to expect.

The heat of the weather was intense to a degree of which I had never formed any I, 64 idea. In / the evening I strove in vain to find a cool breath of air among the trees in the park, or in the streets; I retired to my own room, threw off my clothes, and opened the windows, all to no purpose: I could neither sit, nor walk, nor lie still, without continual perspiration so profuse that I really felt as if nature could not endure it for many hours. This state of oppression will cause little surprise when I inform the reader that in a thorough draft of open air, at eleven o'clock at night, the thermometer stood at 98 degrees of Fahrenheit, a height which I am told it rarely attains under similar circumstances in the most sultry regions in British India.

On the morning of Sunday the 27th, I went to the Episcopalian church of St. Paul, in the Broadway. The service there performed was slightly altered from the English liturgy: some of the alterations are of course necessary, others (such as the curtailing or omitting frequent repetitions) appeared to me judicious, and few, if any, can be censured as departing either in spirit or in tone from the pure model on which they are formed. There was nothing either in the music or in the sermon, to distinguish them from the average of our own churches.

In spite of the extreme heat, I contrived to / lounge for half an hour in Broadway, I, 65 to observe the crowd passing to and from the different places of worship. The dress of the ladies partook generally rather of French than of English costume; and the number of pretty faces and small delicate feet that passed me in that short walk, led me to believe that the encomiums which I had so frequently read upon American beauty were not undeserved. . . .

[In New England]

I, 94 Here I cannot help making a few remarks upon a subject on which I think the general opinion in Britain is erroneous. We are taught to believe that the Yankee is invariably a suspicious and avaricious man in his money transactions, and incapable of those feelings and acts of liberality for which the British character is distinguished. I shall mention two instances that occurred to me in the space of four days, which showed a very different character from that of which New Englanders are accused. The change in the route, which the prevalence of cholera at Montreal induced me to adopt, had prevented me from drawing any of the money which I intended to get in that city, and my finances were, therefore, so much reduced as to leave me only just sufficient to take me as far as Boston. Upon my mentioning the circumstance to Mr. T—, my landlord at Burlington, as my reason for not making some trifling purchases in that town, he at once advanced me fifty dollars, by indorsing my draft on New York, and presenting the bill to the Burlington Bank.

The second instance which I shall quote was in the purchase of the Indian pony.

Mr. C—— of Montpelier, understanding that it would be inconvenient for me to pay his price out of my travelling pocket-money, offered at once to accept my draft on New York for the sum, in which manner the purchase was made. Neither of these gentlemen had ever seen or heard of me before, and neither of them asked even for a letter of introduction or other papers to satisfy them as to any particulars respecting me; and with all due and *modest* allowance for I, 95 my own *gentlemanly* appearance, I very / much doubt whether I should have met with the same liberal treatment, under similar circumstances, at a country town in Yorkshire or Lancashire.

Another thing I am also bound in candour to say, namely, that the descriptions hitherto given by travellers of the accommodations at the taverns in the more remote parts of the country, have been highly coloured to their disadvantage. In travelling for the last fortnight with my own horse and waggon, I have stopped at three or four different places in the course of each day, and have gone through a great portion of the most unsettled country in New York, Vermont, and New Hampshire: in many instances the taverns have been very small; but I have never had reason to complain of want of cleanliness, good victuals, or civility. I have asked, at the most unseasonable hours, both early and late, for breakfast, dinner, and supper; and in the course of ten minutes have always been supplied with a beef steak, potatoes, bread and cheese, butter, eggs, and tea or coffee; the beds have been clean, and whenever I asked for two or three towels instead of the one placed in the room, they have been furnished without any hesitation or extra charge. All that a traveller requires is a sufficient knowledge of the world, to prevent his mistaking manners for intention; and a sufficient fund of good temper in himself to keep him from being irritated by trifles. Upon entering or driving up to a tavern, the landlord will sometimes con- I, 96 tinue / smoking his pipe without noticing your entrance; and if you ask whether you can have dinner, you may be told, "dinner is over, but I guess you can have something." If you are a true John Bull, you will fret and sulk; and silently comparing this with the bustling attention and *empressement* of an English waiter or boots, you walk about by yourself chewing the bitter cud of your wrath; but if you are a traveller, or formed by nature to become one (which John Bull is not), you will take this reception as you find it and as the usage of the country, and in a few minutes *he* of the pipe will be assisting to arrange your baggage, to dry your wet great coat, and a tolerable dinner will be in preparation. Such is the state of things in the North, what it may be in the South and West I have yet to learn. . . .

I, 120 There is nothing more amusing among Americans than the jealous care and assiduity with which they assert and maintain the republican doctrine of equality; while, on the other hand, they observe distinctions and interchange titles which would appear ridiculous in England. For instance, the very first evening that I passed under the roof of my worthy host, not only he, but his farm-assistants and labourers, called me *"Charlie;"* which Christian appellation would doubtless appear very *familiar* to an English ear in the mouth of a person whose acquaintance is just made: the curious observer of character, who wishes to see the *per contra* side of the picture, may find in the first village to which he comes, the small tavern where he lodges kept by a general, the broken wheel of his waggon mended by a colonel, and the day labourers and mechanics speaking of one another as "this gentleman" and "that gentleman."

They will not, probably, continue long to wage this useless war with common sense and the common meaning of words; but will return to the usual acceptation of terms acknowledged by other civilized nations, among whom a general is a man so named from the length or celebrity of his military service, and a gentleman is so called from being, by birth, education, or habits, enabled to follow literary, scientific, or liberal pursuits, which, by refining his manners and enlarging his mind, distinguish him from the great mass of mankind. In short, they cannot change human nature; and in the application of these and similar absurd appellations they must at length find, as a logician might say, that instead of ennobling the subject they only degrade the predicate. Indeed, common candour compels us to confess, that even in Britain the said word "gentleman" has been, like its twin-brother "honour," sadly misapplied; and these high and noble appellations, as they would be understood by a Surrey or a Sidney in olden time, or by kindred minds to theirs in our own, belong with about as much propriety to the coxcomb, the profligate, and the duellist, who assume them among us, as "general" or "gentleman" to the worthy American tavern-keeper or operative. . . .

[In Virginia]

I, 163 From what I had already seen of the social qualities of the gentlemen at whose houses I was a visiter, I was rather gratified than surprised to witness the comparative comfort and good usage enjoyed by their slaves. The huts in which they reside are constructed of wood, and divided in the centre by a compartment, in which is fixed a chimney, to convey the smoke from each division: their food (consisting chiefly of fish, broth, maize, cooked after various fashions, bacon, etc.) is wholesome and sufficient: their clothing coarse, but suited to their necessities and to the climate: their labour compulsory and constant, but not beyond their power. During the days that I spent in the neighbourhood, I did not see any corporal punishment; but each overseer was armed with a cowhide; and one, with whom I held a long conversation regarding the detail of his occupation, informed me that he was obliged constantly to use the lash, both to the men and women: that some he whipped four or five times a week, some only twice or thrice a month: that all attempts to make them I, 164 work regularly / by advice or kindness were unavailing, for their general character was stubborn idleness; and that many who were cheerful, and even appeared attached to the family, would not work without occasional hints from the cowhide. He owned he was extremely sorry that the race existed in Virginia, destroying as they must the market for the white man's labour; adding his conviction that his employer's estate would produce more clear revenue if every negro were removed from the State, and the property divided into farms under lease. The grounds for this opinion, were the heavy original outlay in the purchase of slaves (the price of an able-bodied male being, at an average, 150 pounds) – the expenses of their maintenance – the perpetual losses incurred by their dying, running away, falling sick, and other casualties, the weight of which in free countries falls upon the labourer.

It is doubtless true that all these causes, taken together, render slave-labour less cheap and profitable to the proprietor than it is sometimes assumed to be; but there is also a fact usually advanced by the slaveholders in this district which must not be passed over, and the truth of which cannot be altogether denied, namely, that the banks of the James River are extremely unhealthy during the harvest and hot months, and it is very doubtful whether white labourers (who suffer much more severely than negroes from bilious and other local fevers) could perform the work requisite during / the summer; so that the choice I, 165 must lie between slavery and free-black labour, of which last the Virginians speak as an impracticable theory. That, however, remains to be proved; and as the experiment has been made elsewhere upon a great scale, it is surely more philosophical to wait and observe, rather than conjecture or anticipate the result. The general experience of the past seems to warrant the assertion, that the motives of cleanliness, comfort, and independence are seldom, if ever, strong enough to prevail upon the negro to labour; and that no inducements sufficiently strong can be found excepting necessity and compulsion.

It is to be feared that such will continue to be their character, until it shall have been changed by education and by gradual improvement in their mental and moral condition; indeed, the contrariety of slavery to the laws of nature can scarcely receive stronger confirmation than it does from the fact, that it is necessarily associated with, and dependent for its existence upon, the grossest ignorance and degradation of mind. All civilized nations agree in the great maxims, that knowledge is the power of man — liberty his unalienable right — improvement his object; and yet here is a condition utterly incompatible with the first dawnings of knowledge — the first principles of liberty — the first step in the march of improvement!

I, 166 The abject submission and ignorance *necessary* to the continuance of slavery may be easily gathered from the following statement: — The farms of two gentlemen whom I visited occupied the whole of a peninsula formed by the James River: they had each two overseers; thus (their families being young) the effective strength of white men on their estates amounted to *six:* the negroes were in number about two hundred and fifty: nor was there a village or place within many miles from which assistance could be summoned. Let the reader only imagine the scene that must have ensued had some of these blacks, while smarting under the pain of the lash, been taught the first crude notions of natural right, or been awakened to the first consciousness of their power, or been excited to one feeling of indignation or revenge strong enough to overcome the habitual terror of the cowhide! Hence it is not difficult to understand how justly the slave-holders urge the necessity of keeping from their slaves all glimpses of knowledge or liberty upon the ground of self-preservation; and thus the best apology for slavery furnishes the best evidence of its inhuman unholy nature.

But to return to the plantations on James River. There is a wide difference between the respective conditions of the domestic and the farm-labouring slave; the former has, in many instances, been / brought up under the same roof with his owner — perhaps they have been playmates in early boyhood; he has rarely, if ever, felt the lash; and his respectability of demeanour and attachment to the family are characteristics which it is easy and pleasant to observe; his punishment when idle is generally confined to a scolding, and if that fails, a threat to sell him will almost always reduce the most obstinate to obedience. But the farm-labouring slave is little brought into contact with his master, whose habitual feelings of humanity are, therefore, seldom excited in his favour: he is one of a gang from which, as from a team of horses, a certain quantum of labour is expected; he is entirely at the mercy of the overseer; and the merit of that functionary in the eyes of his employer being to extract the maximum of profit from the exertions of the slaves, he is apt to spare neither threats nor blows in the discharge of his office, and an appeal against him to the master is worse than hopeless, as the negro evidence is unheeded: The complainant, therefore, is well aware that by accusing his oppressor, he would only draw upon himself redoubled severity or cruelty. These overseers are generally men of harsh and unfeeling character, which every day spent in their disagreeable vocation must have a natural tendency to harden; but I have never heard in the South-eastern States of their being guilty of the licentious atrocities of which they have been / sometimes accused in Louisiana, and which certainly are but too common among them in the West India Islands. I, 167 I, 168

The marriage of the slave is, of course, entirely at the option of the owner, by whom it is generally encouraged. If the wife belong to a gang on an adjoining property, the husband is usually allowed to visit her from Saturday night till Monday morning, and sometimes once again in the week from sunset until the following daybreak: the children resulting from the marriage belong to the owner of the mother. The sexual morality of the negroes (being unchecked by any notions of decency or propriety) would be even more lax than it is, were it not restrained by prohibitory regulations on the part of their owners, whose interest it is to prevent all irregularities which might interfere with the labour of the male, or the fecundity of the female slaves: let us hope, also, that some impose these restraints from better and higher motives.

The religion of the negroes is such as might be expected from the brutal state of ignorance in which they are brought up; the dignity, the responsibility, the immortality of man being unknown to them, their religion is a compound of superstition and absurdity, inculcating no virtue, duty, or self-denial, and filling their heads with drivelling fruitless fancies; they always prefer their own preachers (some brother-slave, whose vanity and volubility have induced him to assume the office) to any white minister / that can be offered to them; and the only definite article of belief that I could obtain from several whom I examined, was, that if adultery, theft, and murder were very bad, a few prayers soon expiated the offence, and the "man might start again as good as ever!"

I, 169

The soil on both banks of James River is naturally very fertile; but it has been much exhausted by neglect and by overcropping. A better system of agriculture is now introduced; a triennial rotation is observed, consisting usually of wheat, Indian-corn, and clover; fine beds of marl have lately been discovered of great extent, and the use of this, with shells and a free admixture of animal and vegetable manure, is already producing evident and rapid improvement in the soil and in the crops. Most of the implements of husbandry are made on the farm; the draught cattle consist chiefly of small, lean, but hardy oxen, and stout mules, which are fed upon the coarsest refuse of the produce: thus (with the exception of the value of the slave-labour) the outlay upon these farms is not by any means heavy in proportion to their return; and were it not for the subdivision to which, by the laws of the country, they are so frequently subjected, these estates would maintain a comfortable and independent gentry.

I suppose my American friends would call it British prejudice; but I confess it often made me sad in my journey through Virginia, to see good / substantial manor-houses, built while the law of primogeniture was in force, either untenanted or half-inhabited, because none of the heirs of the subdivided property could afford to live in them. However, although I will not enter further into the merits of that question here, I freely admit that I consider a law of primogeniture incompatible with republican institutions. . . .

I, 170

[In Ohio]

I, 190

I found an amusing contrast in the manners of some western travellers, who were cast in a rougher mould: they were not satisfied till they had found out who I was, where I came from, *why* I came, where I was going to, how long I meant to stay, and, in addition to these particulars, how much my umbrella cost, and what was the price of my hat. This last inquiry was followed by the party taking it up from the bench, and putting it on his *head,* which was not very cool, neither did it appear to have suffered much annoyance from water or from comb; luckily the hat did not fit, and after giving it two or three stout pulls in a vain attempt to draw it over his scalp, he returned it to me. Another fellow saw me smoking a Cabanos cigar; he asked me, "Stranger, have you got another of them things? I will give you a cent for one" (a halfpenny). I immediately gave him one, saying, in perfect good-humour, "I will not sell you one, but I shall be very glad if you will accept this." To my surprise he became irritated and angry, and tried two or three times to force the cent upon me. I refused as stoutly; and at length told him, that if he was determined to buy, and not to accept the cigar, I should charge him half a dollar for it. This view of the case induced him to take it gratis, but he seemed annoyed, and by no means grateful.

I record these curious traits as more or less indicative of the western yeoman: that these sturdy fellows are less civil or good-humoured than those of a similar class in Lancashire or Yorkshire, I neither say nor think; but doubtless their freedom of manner and conduct would be reckoned impertinent in any other country. . . .

I, 203 On the last day of spring I arrived at Cincinnati, that precocious daughter of the West, that seems to have sprung, like the fabled goddess of war and wisdom, into existence in the full panoply of manufacturing and commercial armour. Its situation is admirably chosen both for convenience and beauty, as it stands on a plain gently inclining towards the river; the area of this plain is nearly four miles in diameter, bounded on the north, north-east, and north-west by an undulating well-wooded range of the hills, from the top of which the view of the fertile vale, the city, and the sweeping river, with its broad bosom speckled by steamers and other boats, is one of the loveliest that the eye can desire.

The streets in this city are laid out rectangularly; and thus the eye, in looking along the greater part of them, rests upon the hills before described, which gives a freshness to the prospect rarely to be found in a town. Many of the private houses are large and commodious, and some of them surrounded by pleasant and neatly cultivated gardens; there are about thirty churches, a college, a lunatic asylum, and one for orphans, and other public buildings usually found in a wealthy city.

The museum contains little worthy of notice; moreover, its contents, mean as they are, are miserably deficient in order and arrangement. I was surprised and disappointed, as I had heard much of the valuable collection to be seen in this establishment. There are a few fossil mammoth bones of extraordinary size, and also a number of skulls found in some of the ancient mounds, differing materially in form from those of the modern race of / Indians. **I, 204** There are also several banks and insurance companies, and about twenty periodical publications, three or four of which are daily papers; I also saw one German weekly paper, *Der Deutsche Franklin,* as well written and better printed than most of those which I have seen in the provincial towns in Germany.

The chief article of manufacture (though there are many others of inferior extent), is iron, in every form and shape, especially in the construction of steam-engines. I am told that about one-third of the steamers on the Mississippi and Ohio, amounting, in all, to nearly five hundred, have been built here. The population, as near as I can form a calculation from observation and inquiry, is about forty thousand. They are chiefly composed of emigrants from New England, from Germany, from all parts of the States, and, indeed, of the world.

The building which is the most absurd, ugly, and ridiculous in the town, exhibiting a want of taste and invention only equalled by the contempt which it displays for every rule of architecture, gothic or classic, is the bazaar built by Mrs. Trollope; a lady who did all that lay within the power of her clever and caricaturing pen to hold up the inhabitants of Cincinnati to the ridicule of the civilised world, as regards their manners, their habits, and their taste. This bazaar is a large / nondescript edifice of **I, 205** brick, with a stone, or imitation of stone, face: it has pillars, a cupola, gothic windows, surmounted by Grecian architraves, and scraps of every order (or disorder), from a square brick *box* to an Ionic volute! Neither can I compliment the lady's sagacity any more than her taste; as in this thriving city *her* speculation is probably, the most signal and complete failure that has occurred since its settlement! After losing the greater part of the money embarked in it, she was obliged to leave it unfinished.

As far as my short visit enabled me to judge, her accuracy of description is upon a par with the monuments which she has left here of her speculative sagacity and taste. I have been in company with ten or twelve of the resident families, and have not seen one single instance of rudeness, vulgarity, or incivility; while the shortness of the invitations, and absence of constraint and display, render the society more agreeable, in some respects, than that of more fashionable cities. If the proposition stated is merely this: "that the manners of Cincinnati are not so polished as those of the best circles in London, Paris, or Berlin; that her luxuries, whether culinary or displayed in carriages, houses, or amusements, are also of a lower caste;" I suppose none would be so absurd as to deny it. I hope few would be weak enough gravely to inform the world of so self-evident a truth; but I will, without fear of contradiction, assert, that the history of the world / does not produce a parallel to Cincinnati in rapid growth of wealth and population. Of all the cities that have been founded by mighty sovereigns or nations, with an express view to their becoming the capitals of empires, there is not one that, in twenty-seven years from its foundation, could show such a mass of manufacture, enterprise, population, wealth, and social comfort, as that of which I have given a short and imperfect outline in the last two or three pages; and which owes its magnitude to no adscititious favour or encouragement, but to the judgment with which the situation was chosen, and to the admirable use which its inhabitants have made thereof.

I, 206

When I think of the short period that has elapsed since the red Indian, the bear, the elk, and the buffalo roamed through these hills; since the river (bearing on its bosom nothing but the bark canoe, or the flat-bottomed boat of the Indian trader) flowed in silence through the massive and impenetrable forest; and turn from that fancied picture to the one now before my eyes, displaying crowded and busy streets, rattling with drays and carriages; factories on all sides, resounding with the regular and mighty swing of the engine; numerous taper spires pointing to heaven; thence turn to the river, and see it alive with steaming commerce; and, look beyond over the villages, the neat farms, the orchards, and the gardens – I am filled with astonishment and admiration at the energy / and industry of man, and with pride at the self-suggested reflection, that this metamorphosed wilderness is the work of Britain's sons; and I do pity, from the bottom of my heart, the man (and, above all others, the Englishman) who can see nothing in such a scene but food for unjust comparisons, sneers, raillery, and ridicule!

I, 207

I rode out twice to take a view of the surrounding country. My only acquaintance in the city being with a family whom I had never seen before my arrival, but some members of which I had known at Fayal; and with a Scotch gentleman and his wife, whom I had met at Washington, and who had lately arrived; and yet, with these small means of introduction to society, I received invitations for the evening, several for dinner, and was obliged to decline two or three polite offers of a saddle-horse, from persons to whom I had been only introduced a few hours before. On both occasions when I rode out, I went in company with ladies; and there was nothing in any of the detail of the equipage that would have caused a smile in a riding party in Windsor or Richmond Park, except that the horses are wont to rack or pace – a kind of gait that I think equally ungraceful and disagreeable, but doubtless combining easy motion with tolerable speed.

The gentry in our European cities could not conceive, and could hardly be made to understand, the difficulties in which those of their class find themselves here in regard to servants. The / latter are indeed the most

I, 208

capricious of tyrants. Wealthy and respectable families, instead of their proper complement of servants, are sometimes left with one or two maids in the house, and are unable to give a dinner to their neighbours. Moreover, these said tyrants stay exactly as long as they please, a month, a week, a day, and leave without a moment's warning, sure of finding immediate employment.

On the second morning after my arrival, the proprietor of the tavern in which I lodged went to market, as usual, early, leaving his kitchen full of servants, about to prepare breakfast for one hundred and fifty or two hundred; on his return, he found that the said meal was not forthcoming with its ordinary alacrity; and, on going into his kitchen, discovered that his cook and four of his kitchen-maids had *left* him, none of them having thought it worth while to tell him of their intention. He said they would come or send, in a few days, for their wages, and if they were not immediately paid, would sue him!

My occupations and amusements in Cincinnati were most disagreeably interrupted by a severe attack of cholera. This painful disorder had lately re-appeared in several places in the neighbourhood; and, although its ravages were not so extensive as in the year 1832, they were sufficient to fill the town with alarm, and to cause similar precautionary and sanatory regulations to those I, 209 which / had been before observed. I was for three days under its baneful influence.

On the morning of the second day, after I had gone through the violent depletions which affect the stomach in the first stage of the disorder, the total prostration of strength, and the sharp convulsive cramps which I experienced in my legs, gave reason to believe I should probably not recover. I now dictated and signed a short letter, and a few testamentary particulars, addressed to the British Legation at Washington, adding a superscription, that the seal was not to be broken until the news of my death was confirmed. After this I recollect but little of what passed for some hours. My servant said that my "face was just the colour of lead;" and the physician who attended me told me afterwards, that he gave me in an hour and a half, one hundred and eighty grains of calomel, in three doses of sixty grains each. A sort of lethargy into which I had fallen, was succeded by a more natural sleep; and on the third day, the crisis was passed, and, although exceedingly weak and reduced, I was out of danger.

It would be most ungrateful, were I to forget that I received from the family which I have before mentioned every attention that kindness could dictate or my state admit. The gentleman called on me two or three times a day, sent me from his / house I, 210 a comfortable pillow, wishing to add a better mattress than the one on which I lay; and, moreover, pressed me most earnestly to take up my invalid abode under his roof. There are very few of the older and more luxurious cities where a stranger could expect to meet with similar kindness.

[Kentuckians]

It appears to me, (from the limited opportunities that I have enjoyed for observing) that no two bordering states in the Union differ so much in the character of their population as Ohio and Kentucky. This difference is partially occasioned by the following causes: — First, Kentucky is a slave-state; Ohio is not. Secondly, Ohio was chiefly settled by Germans, New Englanders, a few British, and, in short, an industrious agricultural class; while Kentucky was chiefly settled by the western Virginians, a wild, high-spirited, and somewhat rough tribe of hunters. Thirdly, the soil of the two states tends to the distinction between them, which I have partly attributed to their origin.

Ohio contains probably a higher average of good arable land, compared with its whole extent, than any other state in the Union, so that the bear, the wolf, and even the deer, are almost banished from their woods, and agriculture forms the chief employment of the people; while Kentucky, although boasting of a fine soil, some tracts of great fertility, and a luxuriant growth of timber, has still large portions of country only trodden by the foot of the hunter, and I, 211 that of the various objects of his pursuit. / These causes (probably combined with others which I have omitted) have produced a wide and marked difference of character. The Ohioans are a quiet, industrious, peaceable people, carrying the "republicanism of democracy" (as their German newspaper calls it) to its highest pitch; but too far removed from the scene of action, and not sufficiently congregated in manufacturing or commercial masses, to give to their political feelings the bitterness and personality so prevalent in the East. There is no material difference in the forms of government of the two states, except that in Ohio the government and senators are biennially chosen, whereas in Kentucky they are elected for four years; in both, the House of Representatives is annually elected by what may be called universal suffrage, i.e. every citizen, being twenty-one years of age, and resident in the state.

The character of the Kentuckians has greater merits and greater faults; their moral features are more broadly and distinctly marked. Descended, as I before said, from the western hunters, and some of them from the more wealthy planters of Virginia and North Carolina, they are brave, generous, proud, frank, and hospitable, but apt at the same time to be rough, overbearing, and quarrelsome. They are extremely vain of their State, and inclined to play the braggart, as well in her praises as their own; the former fault, *I*, for one, can freely forgive them, as the want of / I, 212 local or home attachment is one of the least agreeable features of American character. They are, moreover, pretty strongly imbued (probably through their Virginian descent) with a taste for gambling, horse-racing, etc., which is perhaps strengthened by their frequent intercourse on their northern and western frontier with the numerous gamblers, or "sportsmen," who come up the river in spring and summer to avoid the heat and malaria of New Orleans and the adjacent country.

In addition to the above traits of character, there is one of which I cannot speak otherwise than with unqualified reprobation – I mean the cowardly and almost universal practice of carrying a dirk-knife. This instrument, which, like the Italian stiletto, is only fit for the hand of an assassin, is displayed upon every occasion. It has ordinarily a blade about six or eight inches long, sharp on both sides towards the point, and comes out of the handle by a spring, which also prevents its closing on the hand of the owner. I have seen several well-dressed Kentuckians, who would probably think themselves much injured if they were not considered gentlemen of the first grade, picking their teeth with these elegant pocket-companions, in public; and I have repeatedly seen them, while engaged in conversation employ their hands in opening and shutting this dirk-spring, as a London dandy on the stage raps his boots and shakes his watch-seals, or sometimes in *real* life, for want of / I, 213 manual employment, draws his glove on and off, or smooths down the felt of his hat.

Now, I would ask any candid Kentuckian, from what *"chivalrous"* precedent (which epithet they are very fond of applying to themselves), or from what principle, just, noble, or Christian, this habit is derivable? Man is sufficiently irascible, and when angry, prone enough to inflict injury on his fellow creature, without deliberately furnishing himself with a weapon calculated to occasion death, or permanent mutilation, upon the occasion of the slightest dispute or ebullition of temper. . . .

It might be supposed that the coarse and brutal method of fighting, still frequently adopted in this State under the name of "rough and tumble," is sufficiently savage to satisfy the parties concerned. In this, as is well known, they tear one another's hair, bite off noses and ears, gouge out eyes, and,

I, 214 / in short, endeavour to destroy or mutilate each other; but this is not considered sufficient, and Birmingham and Pittsburgh are obliged to complete by the dirk-knife the equipment of the "chivalric Kentuckian." I am fully aware that the stories current respecting "gouging" are exaggerated, and mostly invented; and I am also aware, that many gentlemen, especially among those of advanced age, in Kentucky, disapprove of these practises; but the general argument remains never-the-less untouched; the "rough and tumble" fight is still permitted by the spectators; and if two angry men have one another by the throat, and there is no check upon their fury, either in their own feelings and habits, or in public opinion, the result in any country would be similarly savage. They may formerly have had an excuse for constantly carrying a weapon, when their houses and families were hourly liable to be surprised by the war-whoop of the Indian; but against whom is the dirk-knife now sharpened? against brothers, cousins, and neighbours!

One feature that I have always admired in the English character, and, indeed, have looked upon with *envy*, (as my own countrymen, especially the highlanders, have it not) is their contempt for all lethal weapons, and their honest determined support of fair play in all personal encounters. If a combatant in England were to practise any "rough and tumble" tricks, such as kneeling on a / man's throat or chest when I, 215 on the ground, or gouging, or biting, he would receive a hearty drubbing from the spectators, and conclude the entertainment, (in my opinion, very deservedly) in the nearest horsepond in which he could be immersed. I trust that the progress of civilisation, and increasing weight of a sounder public opinion, will soon put a stop to the custom above censured, which is not confined to Kentucky, but is more or less prevalent in the whole valley of the Mississippi, especially in Louisiana.

THE USE OF THE LIBRARY

This book was designed to enable you to write a term paper from primary source materials which have been collected in this one volume. However, you may later have to write other papers and reports that will require your using the facilities of a library extensively. The resources of a library are so vast and diversified that one must become acquainted with a few basic tools in order to use a library efficiently. The following brief description of the aids that are available in most libraries may prove extremely helpful to you in your search for material on an assigned subject.

One usually begins his search for information by making a tentative bibliography of all books and articles related to his subject. (See the last part of the introduction for a discussion of bibliography.) The experience of many scholars has proved that the most accurate, flexible, and efficient method is to list every item to be consulted on a separate card. This method allows one to add critical and informational notes to each card and to place in a dead file those which prove to be valueless. When the research is completed it is easy to arrange the cards alphabetically for the final bibliography.

Every bibliography card must contain three units of information in complete form — author, title, and facts of publication. It is advisable to place the library call number at the top so the bottom of the card remains open for annotations. The following forms illustrate the most frequent type of entries:

Books

Hanford, James Holly. *A Milton Handbook.* 4th ed. New York: Crofts, 1946.

Wendeborn, Friedrich August. *A View of England Towards the Close of the Eighteenth Century.* Tr. from the original German by the author himself. 2 vols. London (G. G. J. and J. Robinson), 1791.

An article in a journal

Talbert, Ernest W., *et al.* "Recent Literature of the Renaissance." *Studies in Philology,* L (1953), 231–435.

An article or chapter in a book

Wilson, Edmund. "Historical Criticism." *Critiques and Essays in Criticism, 1920–1948.* Ed. Robert W. Stallman. New York: Ronald Press, 1949.

Locating Books

A. Card Catalogue

The chief gateway to the resources of any library is the card catalogue. Every book in the library is represented by at least one card and usually by at least three cards describing the book and giving the call number needed to locate it on the shelves. To use the card catalogue properly one should know a few facts about it.

1. It is actually a three-way bibliography; most books are entered by (1) author, (2) title, and (3) subject.

2. The cards for books written by an author are headed in black type and always

precede the cards for books about an author, which are usually headed in red type.

3. When the name of an author, a subject, and the first word in the title of a book begin with the same word, the author cards are filed first, the subject cards next, and the title cards last. Thus, the cards for books written by authors named Snow will precede the subject cards for books written about snow, which will precede cards for books in which snow is the first word of the title.

4. Every card contains much concise information about a book to help the student evaluate it: the dates of the author's life, the complete title and subtitle, complete facts of publication, number of pages, editions, other subjects under which the book is classified, and the notations about contents, bibliographies, maps, illustrations, and other facts.

5. The subject cards, usually headed in red type, provide a good start toward a bibliography, especially if one pays close attention to the related subjects listed on the cross reference cards, usually headed "see also" and filed after the last subject card. The subjects under which a book is classified are printed near the bottom of many cards and should be regarded as possible cross references.

6. Even though the card catalogue seems to contain everything, it has obvious limitations. It lists only the material found in your library. It does not list the separate essays collected in books and does not list magazine articles. Additional tools must be used if one wants to get the best material available on his subject.

B. Other Guides to Books

1. Bibliographies

The average student has no idea how many bibliographies already exist on almost every conceivable subject. When he uses the card catalogue he should habitually look for the word *bibliography* on the card he examines and for the separate "see also" cards often filed at the end of a group of subject cards. The word *bibliography* on the card means that that particular title contains bibliographies dealing with the same subject as the book; the "see also" card suggests related subjects that might be explored.

The student should remember that most articles in encyclopedias, large dictionaries of biography, and other reference works contain bibliographies. As he reads the books and articles on his list, he should study all footnotes and terminal bibliographies for further suggestions.

He should also try to discover the standard bibliographies in his field. For example, in English literature, most research begins with the *Cambridge Bibliography of English Literature* (CBEL), a definitive work which lists all major studies in English literature published before 1936. Librarians will suggest standard bibliographies in other fields or the student may find them himself by consulting the standard guides to bibliographies:

Bibliographic Index. New York: Wilson, 1938 to date, but the first volume, published in 1938, covers 1937 and 1938.

A valuable listing of current bibliographies in all fields. Published quarterly and cumulated annually.

A World Bibliography of Bibliographies. Ed. Theodore Besterman. Oxford, 1939–40. 2 vols.

Register of National Bibliography. Ed. William P. Courtney. London: Constable, 1905–12. 3 vols.

2. Indexes

Essay and General Literature Index. New York: Wilson, 1934 to date, but the first volume covers 1900–1934.

A guide to essays published in books. Very good for biography, criticism of individual works of an author, and other subjects. For example, the card catalogue does not have a card for each essay contributed to Ronald S. Crane's *Critics and Criticism*, but this index (1952) lists these essays under both subject and author.

Vertical File Service Catalogue. New York: Wilson, 1935 to date, but the first volume covers 1932–1935.

An annotated subject index to pamphlets.

More specialized indexes, such as those to poetry, plays, speeches, songs, short stories, and children's literature, may prove useful, depending on the nature of one's subject.

3. Catalogues

If the student wants to go beyond the resources of his own library or if he wants to determine the price, availability, and other facts about a book, he will probably find the information in a library or book catalogue.

A Catalogue of Books Represented by Library of Congress Printed Cards, issued to July 31, 1942. Ann Arbor Mich.: Edwards Press, 1942–1946.

An author index to the largest library in America. Supplements appear regularly and a subject index to new acquisitions has been published since 1950.

British Museum: *Catalogue of Printed Books.* London: Wm. Clowes, 1881–1900; supplement, 1900–1905.

Primarily an author index. A new *General Catalogue* was started in 1931 and is still in progress.

Cumulative Book Index: A World List of Books in the English Language. New York: Wilson, 1928 to date.

Successor to *United States Catalogue: Books in Print.*

An author, subject, and title index to all copyright books in English. A directory of publishers appears at the end of each volume. To find out whether one of these books is still in print consult the *Publisher's Trade List Annual.*

Locating Magazine Articles

Periodical indexes are as indispensable to the student as the card catalogue because they arrange magazine articles according to the subject discussed, and sometimes by author and title as well. The importance of these indexes lies in the fact that they enable a student to determine in a few minutes whether his subject has been discussed in several hundred different magazines.

A. Periodical Indexes — General

Readers' Guide to Periodical Literature. New York: Wilson, 1905 to date, but the first volume covers 1900–1905.

Author, subject, and occasionally a title index to the more popular periodicals.

International Index to Periodicals. New York: Wilson, 1916 to date, but the first volume covers 1907–1916.

Index to the more scholarly and specialized periodicals, particularly those in humanities and the social sciences. No overlapping with *Readers' Guide.*

Poole's Index to Periodical Literature. Boston: Houghton Mifflin, 1882–1908, but covers 1802–1906.

Must be consulted on any subject which might have been discussed in 19th-century English and American magazines.

B. Periodical Indexes — Special

Every major field of learning has a periodical index of its own. The following is but a partial list.

Public Affairs Information Service. New York: PAIS, 1915 to date.

A subject index to periodicals, books, and pamphlets on economics, political science, and other social sciences.

Industrial Arts Index. New York: Wilson, 1913 to date.

Engineering, business, and trade.

Annual Magazine Subject Index. Boston: Faxon, 1908–1952, but covers 1907–1949.

No duplication of general indexes. Specializes in local history, sport, travel, and the outdoors, and is often bound with a separate dramatic index.

Agricultural Index. New York: Wilson, 1919 to date, but the first volume covers 1916–1919.

Art Index. New York: Wilson, 1933 to date, but the first volume covers 1929–1933.

Education Index. New York: Wilson, 1932 to date, but the first volume covers 1929–1932.

New York Times Index. New York: New York Times, 1913 to date.

An index to the daily news, useful in checking any news event in American newspapers.

Book Review Digest. New York: Wilson, 1906 to date, but the first volume covers 1905–1906.

An analytical list of reviews of books of general interest. Valuable for determining the reliability of a book. The books are arranged by author, but the index lists subject and title. The first entry under each book is usually a summary or a general description. Nearly all books in the *BRD* are listed in the volume corresponding to the copyright date of the first edition, but sometimes one is listed in the volume for the preceding or following year. A subject and title index is cumulated every five years which contains many useful features, such as the heading "fiction" under which all fiction published in the preceding five years is classified in many categories.

Locating Quotations, Allusions, Synopses, and Biographies

A. Concordances

A concordance is an alphabetical index to all the major words in a book, usually the poetic works of an author. By using a concordance one can locate any passage of which he remembers only a word or two. If one has forgotten in which of Keats' poems the line "Beauty is truth, truth Beauty" occurs, he can find the answer by looking up either "truth" or "beauty" in the Keats concordance.

At this date concordances have been published for the Bible and for the poetic works of Browning, Burns, Chaucer, Coleridge, Collins, Cowper, Donne, Fitzgerald, Goldsmith, Gray, Herbert, Herrick, Housman, Keats, Kyd, Marlowe, Milton, Pope, Shakespeare, Shelley, Spenser, Tennyson, Wordsworth, Wyatt; Emerson, Hawthorne, Lanier, Poe, and Whitman.

B. Books of Quotations

To find quotations on a certain subject or to find the author of a quotation, one can get much help from several well-indexed books of quotations, one of which is *Bartlett's Familiar Quotations.* Ed. C. Morley. 12th ed. Boston: Little, 1948.

C. Synopses of Books

Plot summaries of well-known works in fiction and drama are available in many books among which are these:

Reader's Digest of Books. New ed. Ed. Helen R. Keller. New York: Macmillan, 1947.

Master Plots. Ed. Magill and Kohler. New York: Salem Press, 1949–1953.

250 plot summaries in each volume.

Thesaurus of Book Digests: Digest of the World's Permanent Writings from the Ancient Classics to Current Literature. Ed. Hayden and Fuller. New York: Crown, 1949.

D. Handbooks for Readers

An impressive array of general and special one-volume handbooks has been published to provide readers with concise, quickly accessible biographies, synopses, definitions and other useful information. Among the best are these:

Oxford Companion to English Literature. Ed. Paul Harvey. 3rd ed. Oxford, 1946.

Oxford Companion to American Literature. Ed. J. D. Hart. 2nd ed. Oxford, 1948.

Harper's Dictionary to Classical Literature and Antiquities. Ed. H. T. Peck. New York: Am. Book Co., 1923.

A Handbook to Literature. Ed. Thrall and Hibbard. Garden City: Doubleday, Doran, 1936.

A good source for definitions of literary terms.

Reader's Encyclopedia. Ed. W. R. Benét. New York: Crowell, 1948.

Reader's Handbook of Famous Names in Fiction, Allusions, References, Proverbs, Plots, Stories, and Poems. Ed. E. C. Brewer. Philadelphia: Lippincott, 1935.

E. Biographies

1. Historical

Dictionary of National Biography (DNB). Ed. Leslie Stephen and Sidney Lee. London: Smith, Elder; and later, Oxford University Press, 1885–1937. 63 vols. and supplements.

A monumental collection of biographies of all men of any consequence in all walks of life in all periods in English history.

Dictionary of American Biography (DAB). Ed. Allen Johnson and Dumas Malone. New York: Scribner, 1928–1937. 20 vols.

The American companion to the DNB.

Who Was Who. London: Black, 1920 to date. 3 vols.

Biographies of Englishmen who died from 1897–1940.

Who Was Who in America. Chicago: Marquis, 1942.

Biographies of Americans who died from 1897 to 1942.

2. Contemporary

Current Biography: Who's News and Why. New York: Wilson, 1940 to date.

Published monthly and cumulated annually. A master index appears dicennially and in intervening years. Each annual volume contains an index for all preceding volumes.

Biography Index: a Cumulative Index to Biographical Material in Books and Magazines. New York: Wilson, 1946 to date.

Twentieth Century Authors. Ed. S. J. Kunitz. New York: Wilson, 1942.

Biographies and portraits of writers known to English readers.

International Who's Who. London: Europa Publications, 1936 to date.

Who's Who in America. Chicago: Marquis, 1899 to date.

Biennial dictionary of living Americans.

Who's Who. London: Black, 1849 to date.

Primarily British. Published annually.

There are many biographical dictionaries for special fields, such as *Who's Who in the Theatre.*

Other Major Reference Works

A. Encyclopedias (General)

Encyclopaedia Britannica. 14th ed. New York: Encyclopaedia Britannica, Inc., 1929. 24 vols. and supplements. The 9th and 11th editions contained excellent long articles which were continued in the 12th and 13th editions, but in the 14th edition they were broken up and popularized. The index volume of this and other encyclopedias should not be overlooked.

Encyclopedia Americana. 2nd ed. New York: Americana Corporation, 1918–1920. 30 vols. and supplements.

Collier's Encyclopedia. New York: Collier, 1949–1952. 20 vols.

B. Encyclopedias (Special)

Encyclopedia of the Social Sciences. Ed. E. R. A. Seligman and Alvin Johnson. New York: Macmillan, 1930–1935. 15 vols.

An excellent reference work in its field.

Encyclopedia of Religion and Ethics. Ed. James Hastings. New York: Scribner, 1908–1927. 12 vols. and index.

C. Dictionaries

Oxford English Dictionary (OED). Ed. A. H. Murray, *et al.* Oxford, 1888–1933. 13 vols.

The old *New English Dictionary* corrected and re-issued. The most comprehensive English dictionary ever published since it traces the historical changes that have occurred in the meanings, spellings, pronunciations, and usages of English words.

Dictionary of American English on Historical Principles. Ed. Craigie and Hulbert. University of Chicago Press, 1936–1944. 4 vols.

D. Yearbooks and Almanacs

Britannica Book of the Year. 1938 to date.
Annual supplement to the *Encyclopaedia Britannica,* reviewing the year's events and adding new subjects.

American Annual. 1923 to date.
Annual supplement to the *Encyclopedia Americana.*

Statesman's Year-Book. London: Macmillan, 1864 to date.
A reliable guide to the governments of the world.

World Almanac and Book of Facts. New York: World-Telegram, 1868 to date.

E. Atlases and Gazetteers

The Columbia Lippincott Gazetteer of the World. Ed. L. E. Seltzer. Columbia University Press, 1952.

Commercial Atlas. New York: Rand, McNally, 1939 to date.

Historical Atlas. Ed. W. R. Shepherd. 7th ed. New York: Holt, 1929.

Procedure in Preparing a Library Paper

1. Limit your subject. A research paper may require the exhaustive treatment of a limited number of sources or the condensation of extensive materials. Ordinarily you will obtain best results by cutting the subject down as much as possible.

2. Read articles on your subject in the appropriate encyclopedias. This can be discouraging because you may feel that you can add nothing to what you have read. Nevertheless, you will gain by reading the articles. It will give you an overview of your subject and help you decide how much of it to cover in your paper. It may even force you to modify your subject or abandon it entirely. There is no harm in obtaining a few notecards from an encyclopedia article, but it cannot be the major source of information because it is too general. It will provide you with the first materials for your bibliography.

3. Consult the card catalogue, being especially alert to cross references and to notations about bibliographies. Look up the synonyms for key words in your topic. A subject like metrics could be listed under versification or prosody.

4. Consult the standard bibliographies in your field.

5. Consult the periodical indexes, especially those covering the years subsequent to the publication of the bibliographies you used.

6. If you are writing about a person, use the appropriate biographical dictionary.

7. Other suggestions:

a. Read critically. If you have doubts about some of your material, write yourself a warning at the end of a notecard or make a note on the bibliography card.

b. Evaluate your sources by using the *Book Review Digest,* biographical dictionaries, and other reference works. Be on the lookout for internal evidence of reliability or carelessness.

c. Keep an idea card on which you preserve thoughts about organization, conclusions, prefaces, additional sources, etc., that flash across your mind before you can use them.

d. Follow the principles of organization and writing discussed in the introduction to this book.

Suggested Assignments on the Use of the Library

1. Choose ten of the aids listed on pages 104–108 which you consider will be most helpful to you in locating books and magazine articles for use in the writing of research papers. After each of these titles, write in its exact location in the library.

2. Supply the following information about an English or American author. (To avoid the overuse of certain library facilities, the instructor will assign a different author to each student.)

a. Bibliography cards for three books by your author and three books about your author in the card catalogue.

b. The total number of books by your author and about your author in the card catalogue.

c. The number of books about your author which contain bibliographies, according to the card catalogue.

d. The cross references listed on the "see also" card, if one is filed with your author's card.

e. The number of bibliographies about your author listed in two volumes of the *Bibliographic Index.*

f. The number of essays about your author in two volumes of the *Essay and General Literature Index.*

3. Approximately how many magazines are indexed in each of the general periodical indexes and in one of the special periodical indexes?

4. For a subject of your own choice make at least six bibliography cards for articles found in the above periodical indexes. Be sure to write out all abbreviations while the index is before you.

5. This assignment is on the use of the *Book Review Digest.*

a. How many magazines are used as a basis for the *Book Review Digest?*

b. How many classifications are listed under "fiction" in one of the cumulative subject-title indexes?

c. Make correct bibliography cards for several books listed in BRD and indicate the number of favorable, unfavorable, and mixed reviews.

d. Find at least one of the original reviews in your library, list its main points, and compare it with the excerpt in the BRD.

e. Write a paper in which you analyze and summarize all the reviews of a book which you have read.

6. Look up an author of your choosing in the appropriate biographical dictionary and make a résumé of the important facts of his life.

7. Read the biography of a prominent author in a handbook and in a biographical dictionary and report the difference in treatment.

8. Compare the discussion of a recent news event in the two encyclopedia yearbooks.

9. Choose an author and make a bibliography about him by consulting at least three encyclopedias.